The Complete Ninja Foodi Dual Zone Air Fryer Cookbook

1999 Days Quick, Savory and Nutritious Recipes to Air Fry, Bake, Roast and Grill Everyday

Bonnie Klink

Copyright © 2023 by   All rights reserved.

The content contained within this book may not be reproduced, duplicated, or transmitted without direct written permission from the author or the publisher. Under no circumstances will any blame or legal responsibility be held against the publisher, or author, for any damages, reparation, or monetary loss due to the information contained within this book, either directly or indirectly.

Legal Notice: This book is copyright protected. It is only for personal use. You cannot amend, distribute, sell, use, quote or paraphrase any part, or the content within this book, without the consent of the author or publisher.

Disclaimer Notice: Please note the information contained within this document is for educational and entertainment purposes only. All effort has been executed to present accurate, up to date, reliable, complete information. No warranties of any kind are declared or implied. Readers acknowledge that the author is not engaged in the rendering of legal, financial, medical, or professional advice. The content within this book has been derived from various sources. Please consult a licensed professional before attempting any techniques outlined in this book. By reading this document, the reader agrees that under no circumstances is the author responsible for any losses, direct or indirect, that are incurred as a result of the use of the information contained within this document, including, but not limited to, errors, omissions, or inaccuracies.

Table of Contents

Table of Contents 3

Chapter 1: Introduction 7
History of the Ninja Foodi Dual Zone Air Fryer 7
Benefits of the Ninja Foodi Dual Zone Air Fryer 7
Features of the Ninja Foodi Dual Zone Air Fryer 8
Tips for Using the Ninja Foodi Dual Zone Air Fryer 9
Cleaning and Maintenance of the Ninja Foodi Dual Zone Air Fryer 10

Chapter 2: Measurement Conversions 12
BASIC KITCHEN CONVERSIONS & EQUIVALENTS 12

Chapter 3: Snacks And Appetizers Recipes 13
Parmesan French Fries 14
Tasty Sweet Potato Wedges 14
Mozzarella Sticks 14
Tater Tots 15
Mozzarella Balls 15
Fried Cheese 16
Miso-glazed Shishito Peppers Charred Lemon Shishito Peppers 16
Potato Tacos 16
Beef Jerky Pineapple Jerky 17
Shrimp Pirogues 18
Avocado Fries 18
Tofu Veggie Meatballs 18
Ravioli 19
Cauliflower Cheese Patties 19
Lemony Pear Chips 20
Mac And Cheese Balls 20
Air Fried Pot Stickers 21
Crab Rangoon Dip With Crispy Wonton Strips 21
Chicken Stuffed Mushrooms 22
Waffle Fries 22

Chapter 4: Breakfast Recipes 23
Breakfast Pitta 24
Egg And Bacon Muffins 24
Baked Peach Oatmeal 24
Buttermilk Biscuits With Roasted Stone Fruit Compote 25
Baked Mushroom And Mozzarella Frittata With Breakfast Potatoes 25
Bacon, Cheese, And Avocado Melt & Cheesy Scrambled Eggs 26
Bacon And Spinach Egg Muffins 26
Eggs In Avocado Cups 27
Potatoes Lyonnaise 27
Donuts 27
Air Fried Bacon And Eggs 28
Perfect Cinnamon Toast 28
Parmesan Sausage Egg Muffins 29
Crispy Hash Browns 29

Cajun Breakfast Sausage	29
Baked Egg And Mushroom Cups	30
Buffalo Chicken Breakfast Muffins	30
Breakfast Stuffed Peppers	30
Easy Pancake Doughnuts	31
French Toasts	31
Cheesy Baked Eggs	31
Parmesan Ranch Risotto And Oat And Chia Porridge	32
Blueberry Coffee Cake And Maple Sausage Patties	32
Cinnamon Toast	33
Broccoli-mushroom Frittata And Chimichanga Breakfast Burrito	33

Chapter 5: Vegetables And Sides Recipes 35

Brussels Sprouts	36
Acorn Squash Slices	36
Bacon Potato Patties	36
Buffalo Bites	37
Air Fried Okra	37
Caprese Panini With Zucchini Chips	37
Bbq Corn	38
Fried Patty Pan Squash	39
Stuffed Tomatoes	39
Fried Avocado Tacos	39
Green Salad With Crispy Fried Goat Cheese And Baked Croutons	40
Satay-style Tempeh With Corn Fritters	41
Broccoli, Squash, & Pepper	42
Quinoa Patties	42
Buffalo Seitan With Crispy Zucchini Noodles	43

Chapter 6: Beef, Pork, And Lamb Recipes 44

Nigerian Peanut-crusted Bavette Steak	45
Mongolian Beef With Sweet Chili Brussels Sprouts	45
Stuffed Beef Fillet With Feta Cheese	46
Bacon-wrapped Cheese Pork	46
Glazed Steak Recipe	46
Sausage And Cauliflower Arancini	47
Goat Cheese-stuffed Bavette Steak	47
Pigs In A Blanket With Spinach-artichoke Stuffed Mushrooms	48
Beef And Bean Taquitos With Mexican Rice	48
Kielbasa Sausage With Pineapple And Kheema Meatloaf	49
Garlic-rosemary Pork Loin With Scalloped Potatoes And Cauliflower	50
Kheema Burgers	50
Meatballs	51
Easy Breaded Pork Chops	51
Simple Lamb Meatballs	51
Breaded Pork Chops	52
Balsamic Steak Tips With Roasted Asparagus And Mushroom Medley	52
Minute Steak Roll-ups	53
Juicy Pork Chops	53
Steaks With Walnut-blue Cheese Butter	54
Garlic Sirloin Steak	54
Tasty Pork Skewers	54
Mozzarella Stuffed Beef And Pork Meatballs	55

Rosemary And Garlic Lamb Chops ... 55
Sweet And Spicy Country-style Ribs ... 56
Roasted Beef ... 56
Bo Luc Lac ... 56
Blue Cheese Steak Salad ... 57
Bacon Wrapped Pork Tenderloin ... 57
Roast Souvlaki-style Pork With Lemon-feta Baby Potatoes ... 58

Chapter 7: Poultry Recipes ... *59*

Chicken With Pineapple And Peach ... 60
Chicken Caprese ... 60
Chili Chicken Wings ... 60
Apricot-glazed Turkey Tenderloin ... 61
Almond Chicken ... 61
Sweet And Spicy Carrots With Chicken Thighs ... 62
Garlic Parmesan Drumsticks ... 62
Roasted Garlic Chicken Pizza With Cauliflower "wings" ... 62
Turkey Meatloaf With Veggie Medley ... 63
Pretzel Chicken Cordon Bleu ... 64
Crispy Dill Chicken Strips ... 64
Stuffed Chicken Florentine ... 65
Chicken With Bacon And Tomato & Bacon-wrapped Stuffed Chicken Breasts ... 65
Juicy Duck Breast ... 66
Chicken And Vegetable Fajitas ... 66
Curried Orange Honey Chicken ... 66
Air Fried Chicken Potatoes With Sun-dried Tomato ... 67
Spiced Chicken And Vegetables ... 67
Chicken Ranch Wraps ... 68
African Piri-piri Chicken Drumsticks ... 68
Brazilian Chicken Drumsticks ... 69
Wings With Corn On The Cob ... 69
Thai Curry Meatballs ... 70
Cajun Chicken With Vegetables ... 70
Chicken Leg Piece ... 70
Garlic, Buffalo, And Blue Cheese Stuffed Chicken ... 71
Asian Chicken Drumsticks ... 71
"fried" Chicken With Warm Baked Potato Salad ... 72
Asian Chicken ... 72
Chicken Breast Strips ... 73

Chapter 8: Fish And Seafood Recipes ... *74*

Scallops Gratiné With Parmesan ... 75
Orange-mustard Glazed Salmon ... 75
Cajun Catfish Cakes With Cheese ... 75
Lemony Prawns And Courgette ... 76
Flavorful Salmon Fillets ... 76
Bacon Halibut Steak ... 76
Chili Lime Tilapia ... 77
Keto Baked Salmon With Pesto ... 77
Fish Cakes ... 77
Broiled Crab Cakes With Hush Puppies ... 78
Salmon Patties ... 79
"fried" Fish With Seasoned Potato Wedges ... 79

Garlic Butter Salmon 80
Nutty Prawns With Amaretto Glaze 80
Rainbow Salmon Kebabs And Tuna Melt 81
Furikake Salmon 81
Honey Teriyaki Salmon 82
Perfect Parmesan Salmon 82
Steamed Cod With Garlic And Swiss Chard 82
Basil Cheese S·saltalmon 83
Honey Teriyaki Tilapia 83
Cod With Avocado And Garlic Prawns 83
Beer Battered Fish Fillet 84
Easy Herbed Salmon 85
Oyster Po'boy 85
Seafood Shrimp Omelet 85
Crispy Parmesan Cod 86
Pecan-crusted Catfish 86
Salmon Nuggets 87
Buttered Mahi-mahi 87

Chapter 9: Desserts Recipes **88**

Churros 89
Fluffy Layered Peanut Butter Cheesecake Brownies 89
Fried Cheesecake Bites 90
Lemon Sugar Cookie Bars Monster Sugar Cookie Bars 90
Olive Oil Cake & Old-fashioned Fudge Pie 91
Mini Blueberry Pies 91
Walnuts Fritters 91
Jelly Donuts 92
Sweet Protein Powder Doughnut Holes 92
Strawberry Nutella Hand Pies 93
Fruity Blackberry Crisp 93
Victoria Sponge Cake 94
Apple Crumble 94
Dessert Empanadas 95
Chocolate Chip Pecan Biscotti 95
Pumpkin Cookie With Cream Cheese Frosting 96
Stuffed Apples 96
Oreo Rolls 96
Chocolate And Rum Cupcakes 97
Coconut Muffins And Dark Chocolate Lava Cake 97
Baked Brazilian Pineapple 98
Homemade Mint Pie And Strawberry Pecan Pie 98
Homemade Mini Cheesecake 99
S'mores Dip With Cinnamon-sugar Tortillas 99
Grilled Peaches 100

Recipes Index *101*

Chapter 1: Introduction

History of the Ninja Foodi Dual Zone Air Fryer

The Evolution of Air Fryers

Air frying, a revolutionary cooking method, has taken the culinary world by storm in recent years. It's a technique that promises the delicious, crispy results of deep frying but with significantly less oil. However, the roots of air frying can be traced back further than you might think.

The concept of air frying dates back to the early 1900s when French inventor Maxime Ribault patented the "Aerofryer." However, it wasn't until the turn of the 21st century that air fryers began to gain popularity. Philips Electronics introduced one of the first consumer-grade air fryers in 2010, which marked the beginning of a culinary revolution. This innovative appliance used hot air circulation to cook food, requiring only a fraction of the oil used in traditional frying methods.

As the demand for healthier cooking options grew, so did the air fryer market. Companies like Ninja, known for their innovative kitchen appliances, began to explore the possibilities of air frying technology. This led to the development of the Ninja Foodi line of products, including the Ninja Foodi Dual Zone Air Fryer.

Ninja's Innovative Journey

Ninja has earned a reputation for pushing the boundaries of kitchen technology. Their dedication to simplifying and enhancing cooking experiences has made them a household name. Ninja's journey into air frying started with the release of the original Ninja Foodi, a multi-functional appliance that combined pressure cooking, steaming, and air frying capabilities. This appliance revolutionized the way people cooked, offering the convenience of multiple kitchen appliances in one.

Building on the success of the Ninja Foodi, the company continued to innovate. They listened to customer feedback and identified opportunities for improvement. As a result, they introduced the Ninja Foodi Dual Zone Air Fryer, a product that takes air frying to the next level.

The Birth of the Dual Zone Air Fryer

The Ninja Foodi Dual Zone Air Fryer was born out of a desire to provide home cooks with even more versatility and control over their cooking. It is the culmination of years of research and development, and it brings a new level of convenience to the kitchen.

The key innovation in the Ninja Foodi Dual Zone Air Fryer is its dual-zone technology. This feature allows you to independently control two separate cooking zones within the same appliance. You can cook two different foods simultaneously, each with its own temperature and time settings. This means you can prepare a complete meal in one go, saving you time and effort.

In this comprehensive guide, we will delve into the history, benefits, features, and tips for using the Ninja Foodi Dual Zone Air Fryer. By the end, you'll have a thorough understanding of this remarkable kitchen appliance and how to make the most of it in your own culinary adventures.

Benefits of the Ninja Foodi Dual Zone Air Fryer

The Ninja Foodi Dual Zone Air Fryer isn't just another kitchen gadget; it's a game-changer. This section explores the numerous advantages that come with adding this appliance to your kitchen arsenal.

Healthier Cooking

One of the primary benefits of the Ninja Foodi Dual Zone Air Fryer is its ability to cook with significantly less oil than traditional frying methods. Air frying uses hot air to cook food, creating a crispy exterior without the need for excessive oil. This means you can enjoy your favorite fried foods with a fraction of the calories and fat. It's a healthier option for you and your family, making it easier to maintain a balanced diet.

The dual-zone technology also allows you to separate different types of food. You can cook your main dish in one zone and a side of crispy vegetables in the other, all without intermingling flavors or cross-contaminating ingredients. This versatility makes it easier to accommodate dietary restrictions and preferences.

Versatile Cooking Options

The Ninja Foodi Dual Zone Air Fryer isn't limited to just frying. It's a versatile kitchen companion that can handle a wide range of cooking tasks. Here are some of the many cooking methods you can explore with this appliance:

Air Frying: As the name suggests, air frying is the Ninja Foodi Dual Zone Air Fryer's specialty. It crisps up food using hot air circulation, creating that desirable crunch without excess oil.

Roasting: Use the air fryer to roast vegetables, meats, or even whole chickens. The even heat distribution ensures that your dishes are perfectly cooked and browned.

Baking: You can bake everything from cookies to muffins in the Ninja Foodi Dual Zone Air Fryer. The precise temperature control ensures consistent results.

Dehydrating: Make your own healthy snacks by dehydrating fruits, vegetables, or even jerky. It's a cost-effective way to enjoy your favorite dried foods without the additives found in store-bought versions.

Reheating: Reheat leftovers to perfection. The dual-zone technology allows you to reheat different foods at different temperatures simultaneously.

Grilling: With the addition of the grill grate accessory, you can achieve grill-like marks and flavors on your food without the hassle of firing up an outdoor grill.

Time-Saving Convenience

Cooking with the Ninja Foodi Dual Zone Air Fryer is not only healthier but also more convenient. It heats up quickly, so you can start cooking your meals faster than traditional ovens or stovetops. Additionally, the dual-zone feature means you can prepare multiple dishes at once, saving you valuable time in the kitchen.

The appliance's smart cooking functions and pre-programmed settings take the guesswork out of cooking. Whether you're air frying, roasting, or baking, you can rely on the Ninja Foodi Dual Zone Air Fryer to deliver consistent and delicious results.

Energy Efficiency

Compared to using a conventional oven or stovetop, the Ninja Foodi Dual Zone Air Fryer is more energy-efficient. Its compact size and rapid heating mean it uses less energy to cook your meals. Plus, you won't need to preheat the entire oven for small cooking tasks, which further reduces energy consumption.

By harnessing the power of hot air circulation, this appliance cooks food evenly and efficiently. It's not only good for your energy bills but also for the environment.

In the next chapter, we will delve into the features that make the Ninja Foodi Dual Zone Air Fryer stand out and enhance your cooking experience.

Features of the Ninja Foodi Dual Zone Air Fryer

The Ninja Foodi Dual Zone Air Fryer is packed with innovative features that set it apart from other kitchen appliances. Let's explore these features in detail to understand how they contribute to an exceptional cooking experience.

Dual Zone Technology

The standout feature of the Ninja Foodi Dual Zone Air Fryer is its dual-zone technology. This technology allows you to use two independent cooking zones within the same appliance. Each zone has its own heating element and fan, enabling you to cook two different dishes simultaneously at different temperatures and times. Imagine cooking chicken wings in one zone while air frying a batch of crispy french fries in the other. With the Ninja Foodi Dual Zone Air Fryer, you can achieve this without any flavor transfer or mixing of cooking odors. It's like having two air fryers in one, making meal preparation more efficient and enjoyable.

Cooking Capacity

This air fryer comes with a generous cooking capacity, allowing you to prepare meals for the whole family or a group of friends. The dual-zone design provides a total of 8-quarts of cooking space, which is divided into two zones. Each zone can hold a substantial amount of food, making it easy to cook large meals or multiple dishes at once.

Whether you're hosting a dinner party or simply making a weeknight dinner, the Ninja Foodi Dual Zone Air Fryer has the capacity to handle your culinary needs. It can accommodate everything from whole chickens to large batches of appetizers, ensuring you have enough food for everyone.

Smart Cooking Functions

The Ninja Foodi Dual Zone Air Fryer features several smart cooking functions that simplify meal preparation. These pre-programmed settings are designed to take the guesswork out of cooking, ensuring that your dishes come out perfectly every time. Some of the smart cooking functions include:

Air Fry: Perfect for achieving crispy, golden-brown results with minimal oil.
Roast: Use this function for even cooking and browning of meats and vegetables.
Bake: Whether you're making cookies or bread, the bake function ensures consistent results.
Reheat: Quickly and evenly reheat leftovers without drying them out.
Dehydrate: Make your own dried fruits, herbs, and more with the dehydrate function.
Customize: Adjust time and temperature settings to suit your specific recipes and preferences.

These smart functions make it easy for beginners and experienced cooks alike to use the Ninja Foodi Dual Zone Air Fryer with confidence.

Precision Temperature Control

Cooking often requires precise temperature control, especially when baking or roasting. The Ninja Foodi Dual Zone Air Fryer offers temperature settings that range from 105°F to 450°F (40°C to 230°C), allowing you to fine-tune the cooking process to achieve the desired results. The ability to set specific temperatures ensures that your dishes are cooked to perfection, whether you're searing a steak or baking delicate pastries.

Easy-to-Use Control Panel

The control panel of the Ninja Foodi Dual Zone Air Fryer is designed for user-friendliness. It features an intuitive interface with clearly labeled buttons and a digital display. Navigating through cooking options, adjusting settings, and selecting cooking functions is straightforward, even for those who are new to air frying technology.

Safety Features

Safety is a top priority when it comes to kitchen appliances, and the Ninja Foodi Dual Zone Air Fryer doesn't disappoint. It's equipped with multiple safety features to ensure worry-free cooking. Some of these safety measures include:

Auto Shut-Off: The appliance will automatically turn off when the cooking time is complete, preventing overcooking or accidents.
Cool-Touch Exterior: The outer surface of the air fryer remains cool to the touch during operation, reducing the risk of burns.
Dishwasher-Safe Parts: Many of the removable parts are dishwasher safe, making cleanup easy and safe.

Now that we've explored the features of the Ninja Foodi Dual Zone Air Fryer, you have a better understanding of what makes this appliance so exceptional. In the next chapter, we'll provide valuable tips for using it to achieve the best cooking results.

Tips for Using the Ninja Foodi Dual Zone Air Fryer

To truly master the art of cooking with the Ninja Foodi Dual Zone Air Fryer, it's essential to know some tips and techniques that will help you make the most of this versatile appliance. Here are some expert tips to ensure your air frying endeavors are a resounding success:

Preheating the Air Fryer

Preheating is an essential step when using the Ninja Foodi Dual Zone Air Fryer, just like with a conventional oven. Preheating helps to ensure that the cooking chamber is at the desired temperature before you place your food inside. Follow these steps to preheat your air fryer:

Ensure the air fryer is plugged in and the power is turned on.

Set the desired temperature and cooking time for preheating, typically at the cooking temperature for your recipe.

Press the "Start" button to begin the preheating process.

Wait for the air fryer to reach the set temperature. It will indicate when it's ready to use.

Preheating helps with even cooking and ensures that your food cooks properly from the start.

Proper Food Placement

How you arrange your food inside the air fryer basket can significantly impact the cooking results. Follow these guidelines for proper food placement:

Don't Overcrowd: Avoid overcrowding the basket. Give your food some space to allow hot air to circulate evenly around each piece. Overcrowding can lead to uneven cooking.

Use Racks and Accessories: The Ninja Foodi Dual Zone Air Fryer often comes with racks and accessories that can help you cook multiple layers of food simultaneously. Utilize these to maximize your cooking capacity.

Use Cooking Oil Sparingly: While one of the benefits of air frying is using less oil, a light mist of oil on your food can enhance the crispiness. Use an oil sprayer to evenly distribute a small amount of oil before cooking.

Cooking Times and Temperatures

Different foods require different cooking times and temperatures. While the Ninja Foodi Dual Zone Air Fryer offers a variety of preset cooking functions, it's essential to know the basics of cooking times and temperatures for common foods. Here are some general guidelines:

Frying: Most foods that you would traditionally fry can be air fried at around 350°F (175°C). Cook until they reach your desired level of crispiness.

Roasting: Roasting vegetables or meats typically requires higher temperatures, often in the range of 375°F to 425°F (190°C to 220°C). The cooking time depends on the specific item and size.

Baking: Baking goods like cookies and bread usually require a lower temperature, around 325°F (160°C), and a longer cooking time.

Dehydrating: For dehydrating fruits or herbs, set the temperature to the lowest setting, usually around 105°F to 115°F (40°C to 46°C), and allow for several hours of drying time.

Always refer to your specific recipe for exact temperature and time recommendations, as they can vary based on ingredients and personal preferences.

Mixing and Shaking

For foods that require turning or flipping during cooking, it's essential to do so to ensure even browning. Here's how to manage this:

Shake the Basket: Many air fryer recipes will instruct you to shake the basket or flip the food halfway through cooking. This action helps distribute heat evenly and ensures that both sides of your food are crispy and delicious.

Use Tongs or a Spatula: When flipping individual items like chicken wings or fries, use tongs or a spatula to turn them over gently.

Experimenting with Recipes

The Ninja Foodi Dual Zone Air Fryer is a versatile appliance that invites creativity in the kitchen. Don't be afraid to experiment with different recipes and ingredients. You can use it to cook a wide range of dishes, from classic comfort foods to healthier options. Here are some ideas to get you started:

Classic French Fries: Achieve crispy, golden-brown fries with minimal oil.

Crispy Chicken Wings: Coat them in your favorite sauces for a delicious appetizer.

Roasted Vegetables: Elevate your side dishes with perfectly roasted veggies.

Homemade Pizza: Make personal-sized pizzas with your favorite toppings.

Breaded Seafood: Try air-frying shrimp or fish for a healthier alternative to deep frying.

Healthy Snacks: Dehydrate fruits, make kale chips, or roast chickpeas for nutritious snacks.

Desserts: Bake cookies, brownies, or mini cakes for a sweet treat.

By experimenting with different recipes, you'll discover the full potential of your Ninja Foodi Dual Zone Air Fryer and uncover new culinary delights.

Cleaning and Maintenance of the Ninja Foodi Dual Zone Air Fryer

Proper cleaning and maintenance of your Ninja Foodi Dual Zone Air Fryer are essential to ensure its longevity and optimal performance. Neglecting this aspect can lead to a buildup of residue, affecting the flavor of your food and the efficiency of the appliance. Here's a step-by-step guide on how to clean and maintain your air fryer:

Cleaning After Each Use

Unplug the Air Fryer: Before cleaning, always make sure the air fryer is unplugged and has cooled down.

Remove Removable Parts: Carefully remove the air fryer basket, crisper plate, and any other removable components. These parts are usually dishwasher safe, so you can place them in the dishwasher for easy cleaning.

Wipe Down the Exterior: Use a damp cloth or sponge

to clean the exterior of the air fryer, including the control panel and the outer housing. Be cautious not to let any water enter the appliance.

Clean the Interior: Use a non-abrasive sponge or brush to clean the interior of the air fryer, including the heating element and the inside walls. Stubborn residue can be removed with a mixture of warm water and a mild dishwashing detergent. Be sure to rinse thoroughly and dry completely before reassembling.

Empty and Clean the Drip Tray: Remove and empty the drip tray, which collects any excess oil or grease. Wash it with warm, soapy water, rinse, and dry thoroughly.

Deep Cleaning

Perform a deep clean of your Ninja Foodi Dual Zone Air Fryer regularly to prevent the buildup of grease and food residue that can affect the flavor of your dishes.

Unplug the Air Fryer: Ensure the appliance is unplugged and completely cooled down.

Disassemble the Air Fryer: Remove all removable parts, including the air fryer basket, crisper plate, and drip tray.

Clean the Heating Element: Use a brush or a soft cloth to clean the heating element carefully. Be gentle to avoid damaging it.

Clean the Inside Walls: Wipe down the inside walls of the air fryer with a damp cloth or sponge. For stubborn residue, use a mixture of warm water and a mild dishwashing detergent.

Clean the Exterior: Clean the exterior of the air fryer, including the control panel and the outer housing, with a damp cloth or sponge.

Clean the Accessories: If the accessories are dishwasher safe, run them through a dishwasher cycle. If not, wash them by hand with warm, soapy water, rinse, and dry thoroughly.

Reassemble the Air Fryer: Once all the components are clean and dry, reassemble the air fryer.

Store Properly: When not in use, store the air fryer in a cool, dry place, preferably with the cord neatly wrapped and stored.

Maintenance Tips

To keep your Ninja Foodi Dual Zone Air Fryer in top condition, consider these maintenance tips:

Check for Damaged Parts: Regularly inspect the heating element, power cord, and other components for signs of damage or wear. If you notice any issues, contact the manufacturer for repairs or replacements.

Replace Filters: Some air fryers have filters that help reduce odors. Check if your model has a filter and replace it as recommended in the user manual.

Oil Management: Empty and clean the drip tray after each use to prevent oil buildup and potential fire hazards.

Avoid Abrasive Cleaners: Never use abrasive scrubbers or harsh cleaning agents on the air fryer, as they can damage the nonstick coating and other surfaces.

Follow User Manual Guidelines: Always refer to the user manual for specific cleaning and maintenance instructions for your Ninja Foodi Dual Zone Air Fryer model.

Troubleshooting Common Issues

If you encounter any issues with your Ninja Foodi Dual Zone Air Fryer, consult the troubleshooting section of the user manual. Common issues may include uneven cooking, unusual noises, or error codes on the control panel. Many problems can be resolved by following the manufacturer's guidance.

In conclusion, the Ninja Foodi Dual Zone Air Fryer is a remarkable kitchen appliance that offers numerous benefits, including healthier cooking, versatile options, time-saving convenience, and energy efficiency. Its innovative features, such as dual-zone technology and smart cooking functions, make it a valuable addition to any kitchen. By following our expert tips for using and maintaining your air fryer, you can enjoy delicious meals and snacks with ease while prolonging the life of your appliance.

Whether you're a novice cook looking to simplify meal preparation or a seasoned chef eager to explore new culinary horizons, the Ninja Foodi Dual Zone Air Fryer empowers you to create culinary delights with

confidence and convenience. So, dive into the world of air frying and discover the endless possibilities this innovative appliance has to offer.

Chapter 2: Measurement Conversions

BASIC KITCHEN CONVERSIONS & EQUIVALENTS

DRY MEASUREMENTS CONVERSION CHART
3 TEASPOONS = 1 TABLESPOON = 1/16 CUP
6 TEASPOONS = 2 TABLESPOONS = 1/8 CUP
12 TEASPOONS = 4 TABLESPOONS = 1/4 CUP
24 TEASPOONS = 8 TABLESPOONS = 1/2 CUP
36 TEASPOONS = 12 TABLESPOONS = 3/4 CUP
48 TEASPOONS = 16 TABLESPOONS = 1 CUP

METRIC TO US COOKING CONVERSIONS
OVEN TEMPERATURES
120 °C = 250 °F
160 °C = 320 °F
180° C = 360 °F
205 °C = 400 °F
220 °C = 425 °F

LIQUID MEASUREMENTS CONVERSION CHART
8 FLUID OUNCES = 1 CUP = 1/2 PINT = 1/4 QUART
16 FLUID OUNCES = 2 CUPS = 1 PINT = 1/2 QUART
32 FLUID OUNCES = 4 CUPS = 2 PINTS = 1 QUART = 1/4 GALLON
128 FLUID OUNCES = 16 CUPS = 8 PINTS = 4 QUARTS = 1 GALLON

BAKING IN GRAMS
1 CUP FLOUR = 140 GRAMS
1 CUP SUGAR = 150 GRAMS
1 CUP POWDERED SUGAR = 160 GRAMS
1 CUP HEAVY CREAM = 235 GRAMS

VOLUME
1 MILLILITER = 1/5 TEASPOON
5 ML = 1 TEASPOON
15 ML = 1 TABLESPOON
240 ML = 1 CUP OR 8 FLUID OUNCES
1 LITER = 34 FL. OUNCES

WEIGHT
1 GRAM = .035 OUNCES
100 GRAMS = 3.5 OUNCES
500 GRAMS = 1.1 POUNDS
1 KILOGRAM = 35 OUNCES

US TO METRIC COOKING CONVERSIONS
1/5 TSP = 1 ML
1 TSP = 5 ML
1 TBSP = 15 ML
1 FL OUNCE = 30 ML
1 CUP = 237 ML
1 PINT (2 CUPS) = 473 ML
1 QUART (4 CUPS) = .95 LITER
1 GALLON (16 CUPS) = 3.8 LITERS
1 OZ = 28 GRAMS
1 POUND = 454 GRAMS

BUTTER
1 CUP BUTTER = 2 STICKS = 8 OUNCES = 230 GRAMS = 8 TABLESPOONS

WHAT DOES 1 CUP EQUAL
1 CUP = 8 FLUID OUNCES
1 CUP = 16 TABLESPOONS
1 CUP = 48 TEASPOONS
1 CUP = 1/2 PINT
1 CUP = 1/4 QUART
1 CUP = 1/16 GALLON
1 CUP = 240 ML

BAKING PAN CONVERSIONS
1 CUP ALL-PURPOSE FLOUR = 4.5 OZ
1 CUP ROLLED OATS = 3 OZ 1 LARGE EGG = 1.7 OZ
1 CUP BUTTER = 8 OZ 1 CUP MILK = 8 OZ
1 CUP HEAVY CREAM = 8.4 OZ
1 CUP GRANULATED SUGAR = 7.1 OZ
1 CUP PACKED BROWN SUGAR = 7.75 OZ
1 CUP VEGETABLE OIL = 7.7 OZ
1 CUP UNSIFTED POWDERED SUGAR = 4.4 OZ

BAKING PAN CONVERSIONS
9-INCH ROUND CAKE PAN = 12 CUPS
10-INCH TUBE PAN = 16 CUPS
11-INCH BUNDT PAN = 12 CUPS
9-INCH SPRINGFORM PAN = 10 CUPS
9 X 5 INCH LOAF PAN = 8 CUPS
9-INCH SQUARE PAN = 8 CUPS

Chapter 3: Snacks And Appetizers Recipes

Parmesan French Fries

Servings: 6
Cooking Time: 20 Minutes.

Ingredients:
- 3 medium russet potatoes
- 2 tablespoons parmesan cheese
- 2 tablespoons fresh parsley, chopped
- 1 tablespoon olive oil
- Salt, to taste

Directions:
1. Wash the potatoes and pass them through the fries' cutter to get ¼-inch-thick fries.
2. Place the fries in a colander and drizzle salt on top.
3. Leave these fries for 10 minutes, then rinse.
4. Toss the potatoes with parmesan cheese, oil, salt, and parsley in a bowl.
5. Divide the potatoes into the two crisper plates.
6. Return the crisper plates to the Ninja Foodi Dual Zone Air Fryer.
7. Choose the Air Fry mode for Zone 1 and set the temperature to 360 degrees F and the time to 20 minutes.
8. Select the "MATCH" button to copy the settings for Zone 2.
9. Initiate cooking by pressing the START/STOP button.
10. Toss the chips once cooked halfway through, then resume cooking.
11. Serve warm.

Nutrition:
- (Per serving) Calories 307 | Fat 8.6g |Sodium 510mg | Carbs 22.2g | Fiber 1.4g | Sugar 13g | Protein 33.6g

Tasty Sweet Potato Wedges

Servings: 4
Cooking Time: 20 Minutes

Ingredients:
- 2 sweet potatoes, peel & cut into wedges
- 1 tbsp BBQ spice rub
- ½ tsp sweet paprika
- 1 tbsp olive oil
- Pepper
- Salt

Directions:
1. In a bowl, toss sweet potato wedges with sweet paprika, oil, BBQ spice rub, pepper, and salt.
2. Insert a crisper plate in the Ninja Foodi air fryer baskets.
3. Add sweet potato wedges in both baskets.
4. Select zone 1 then select "air fry" mode and set the temperature to 390 degrees F for 20 minutes. Press "match" to match zone 2 settings to zone 1. Press "start/stop" to begin. Turn halfway through.

Nutrition:
- (Per serving) Calories 87 | Fat 3.6g |Sodium 75mg | Carbs 13.2g | Fiber 2.1g | Sugar 2.8g | Protein 1.1g

Mozzarella Sticks

Servings: 8
Cooking Time: 1 Hour 15 Minutes

Ingredients:
- 8 mozzarella sticks
- ¼ cup all-purpose flour
- 1 egg, whisked
- 1 cup panko breadcrumbs
- ½ teaspoon each onion powder, garlic powder, smoked paprika, salt

Directions:
1. Freeze the mozzarella sticks for 30 minutes after placing them on a parchment-lined plate.
2. In the meantime, set up your "breading station": Fill a Ziploc bag halfway with flour. In a small dish, whisk the egg. In a separate shallow bowl, combine the panko and spices.

3. To bread your mozzarella sticks: Toss the sticks into the bag of flour, seal it, and shake to coat the cheese evenly. Take out the sticks and dip them in the egg, then in the panko, one at a time. Put the coated sticks back on the plate and put them in the freezer for another 30 minutes.
4. Place a crisper plate in each drawer, then add the mozzarella sticks in a single layer to each. Insert the drawers into the unit.
5. Select zone 1, then AIR FRY, then set the temperature to 400 degrees F/ 200 degrees C with a 15-minute timer. To match zone 2 settings to zone 1, choose MATCH. To begin, select START/STOP

Nutrition:
- (Per serving) Calories 131 | Fat 5.3g | Sodium 243mg | Carbs 11.3g | Fiber 1.1g | Sugar 0.3g | Protein 9.9g

Tater Tots

Servings: 4
Cooking Time: 8 Minutes

Ingredients:
- 16 ounces tater tots
- ½ cup shredded cheddar cheese
- 1½ teaspoons bacon bits
- 2 green onions, chopped
- Sour cream (optional)

Directions:
1. Place a crisper plate in each drawer. Put the tater tots into the drawers in a single layer. Insert the drawers into the unit.
2. Select zone 1, then AIR FRY, then set the temperature to 360 degrees F/ 180 degrees C with a 6-minute timer. To match zone 2 settings to zone 1, choose MATCH. To begin, select START/STOP.
3. When the cooking time is over, add the shredded cheddar cheese, bacon bits, and green onions over the tater tots. Select zone 1, AIR FRY, 360 degrees F/ 180 degrees C, for 4 minutes. Select MATCH. Press START/STOP.
4. Drizzle sour cream over the top before serving.
5. Enjoy!

Nutrition:
- (Per serving) Calories 335 | Fat 19.1g | Sodium 761mg | Carbs 34.1g | Fiber 3g | Sugar 0.6g | Protein 8.9g

Mozzarella Balls

Servings: 6
Cooking Time: 13 Minutes

Ingredients:
- 2 cups mozzarella, shredded
- 3 tablespoons cornstarch
- 3 tablespoons water
- 2 eggs, beaten
- 1 cup Italian seasoned breadcrumbs
- 1 tablespoon Italian seasoning
- 1½ teaspoons garlic powder
- 1 teaspoon salt
- 1½ teaspoons Parmesan

Directions:
1. Mix mozzarella with parmesan, water and cornstarch in a bowl.
2. Make 1-inch balls out of this mixture.
3. Mix breadcrumbs with seasoning, salt, and garlic powder in a bowl.
4. Dip the balls into the beaten eggs and coat with the breadcrumbs.
5. Place the coated balls in the air fryer baskets.
6. Return the air fryer basket 1 to Zone 1, and basket 2 to Zone 2 of the Ninja Foodi 2-Basket Air Fryer.
7. Choose the "Air Fry" mode for Zone 1 and set the temperature to 360 degrees F and 13 minutes of cooking time.
8. Select the "MATCH COOK" option to copy the settings for Zone 2.
9. Initiate cooking by pressing the START/PAUSE BUTTON.
10. Toss the balls once cooked halfway through.
11. Serve.

Nutrition:
- (Per serving) Calories 307 | Fat 8.6g | Sodium 510mg | Carbs 22.2g | Fiber 1.4g | Sugar 13g | Protein 33.6g

Fried Cheese

Servings: 4
Cooking Time: 12 Minutes
Ingredients:
- 1 Mozzarella cheese block, cut into sticks
- 2 teaspoons olive oil

Directions:
1. Divide the cheese slices into the Ninja Foodi 2 Baskets Air Fryer baskets.
2. Drizzle olive oil over the cheese slices.
3. Return the air fryer basket 1 to Zone 1, and basket 2 to Zone 2 of the Ninja Foodi 2-Basket Air Fryer.
4. Choose the "Air Fry" mode for Zone 1 and set the temperature to 360 degrees F and 12 minutes of cooking time.
5. Flip the cheese slices once cooked halfway through.
6. Serve.

Nutrition:
- (Per serving) Calories 186 | Fat 3g | Sodium 223mg | Carbs 31g | Fiber 8.7g | Sugar 5.5g | Protein 9.7g

Miso-glazed Shishito Peppers Charred Lemon Shishito Peppers

Servings: 4
Cooking Time: 10 Minutes
Ingredients:
- FOR THE MISO-GLAZED PEPPERS
- 2 tablespoons vegetable oil
- 2 tablespoons water
- 1 tablespoon white miso
- 1 teaspoon grated fresh ginger
- ½ pound shishito peppers
- FOR THE CHARRED LEMON PEPPERS
- ½ pound shishito peppers
- 1 lemon, cut into ⅛-inch-thick rounds
- 2 garlic cloves, minced
- 2 tablespoons vegetable oil
- ½ teaspoon kosher salt

Directions:
1. To prep the miso-glazed peppers: In a large bowl, mix the vegetable oil, water, miso, and ginger until well combined. Add the shishitos and toss to coat.
2. To prep the charred lemon peppers: In a large bowl, combine the shishitos, lemon slices, garlic, vegetable oil, and salt. Toss to coat.
3. To cook the peppers: Install a crisper plate in each of the two baskets. Place the miso-glazed peppers in the Zone 1 basket and insert the basket in the unit. Place the peppers with lemons in the Zone 2 basket and insert the basket in the unit.
4. Select Zone 1, select AIR FRY, set the temperature to 390°F, and set the time to 10 minutes. Select MATCH COOK to match Zone 2 settings to Zone 1.
5. Press START/PAUSE to begin cooking.
6. When both timers read 4 minutes, press START/PAUSE. Remove both baskets and shake well. Reinsert the baskets and press START/PAUSE to resume cooking.
7. When cooking is complete, serve immediately.

Nutrition:
- (Per serving) Calories: 165; Total fat: 14g; Saturated fat: 2g; Carbohydrates: 9g; Fiber: 2g; Protein: 2g; Sodium: 334mg

Potato Tacos

Servings: 6
Cooking Time: 15 Minutes
Ingredients:
- 5 small russet potatoes
- 24 mini corn tortillas
- 2 tablespoons rapeseed oil
- ½ teaspoon ground cumin
- ½ teaspoon smoked paprika
- ½ teaspoon granulated garlic

- Salt and pepper, to taste
- 24 long toothpicks

Directions:
1. Fill a pot halfway with cold water and add entire potatoes. Bring to a boil over high heat, then reduce to medium-high and simmer until fork-tender, about 15 minutes.
2. It takes about 15-20 minutes. Drain and allow to cool slightly before peeling.
3. In a bowl, combine peeled potatoes and seasonings. Mash until the mixture is relatively smooth. Season to taste.
4. Heat tortillas in a large frying pan until warm and malleable. Cover with a towel while you finish heating the rest of the tortillas.
5. On half of a tortilla, spread roughly one heaping tablespoon of mash. Fold it in half and weave a toothpick through it to seal it.
6. Brush the tacos lightly with oil on both sides.
7. Press your chosen zone - "Zone 1" or "Zone 2" and then rotate the knob to select "Air Fryer".
8. Set the temperature to 200 degrees C, and then set the time for 5 minutes to preheat.
9. After preheating, arrange them into the basket of each zone.
10. Slide the baskets into Air Fryer and set the time for 15 minutes.
11. After cooking time is completed, place on a wire rack for a few minutes, then transfer onto serving plates and serve.

Beef Jerky Pineapple Jerky

Servings: 8
Cooking Time: 6 To 12 Hours

Ingredients:
- FOR THE BEEF JERKY
- ½ cup reduced-sodium soy sauce
- ¼ cup pineapple juice
- 1 tablespoon dark brown sugar
- 1 tablespoon Worcestershire sauce
- ½ teaspoon smoked paprika
- ¼ teaspoon freshly ground black pepper
- ¼ teaspoon red pepper flakes
- 1 pound beef bottom round, trimmed of excess fat, cut into ¼-inch-thick slices
- FOR THE PINEAPPLE JERKY
- 1 pound pineapple, cut into ⅛-inch-thick rounds, pat dry
- 1 teaspoon chili powder (optional)

Directions:
1. To prep the beef jerky: In a large zip-top bag, combine the soy sauce, pineapple juice, brown sugar, Worcestershire sauce, smoked paprika, black pepper, and red pepper flakes.
2. Add the beef slices, seal the bag, and toss to coat the meat in the marinade. Refrigerate overnight or for at least 8 hours.
3. Remove the beef slices and discard the marinade. Using a paper towel, pat the slices dry to remove excess marinade.
4. To prep the pineapple jerky: Sprinkle the pineapple with chili powder (if using).
5. To dehydrate the jerky: Arrange half of the beef slices in a single layer in the Zone 1 basket, making sure they do not overlap. Place a crisper plate on top of the beef slices and arrange the remaining slices in a single layer on top of the crisper plate. Insert the basket in the unit.
6. Repeat this process with the pineapple in the Zone 2 basket and insert the basket in the unit.
7. Select Zone 1, select DEHYDRATE, set the temperature to 150°F, and set the time to 8 hours.
8. Select Zone 2, select DEHYDRATE, set the temperature to 135°F, and set the time to 12 hours.
9. Press START/PAUSE to begin cooking.
10. When the Zone 1 timer reads 2 hours, press START/PAUSE. Remove the basket and check the beef jerky for doneness. If necessary, reinsert the basket and press START/PAUSE to resume cooking.

Nutrition:
- (Per serving) Calories: 171; Total fat: 6.5g; Saturated fat: 2g; Carbohydrates: 2g; Fiber: 0g; Protein: 25g; Sodium: 369mg

Shrimp Pirogues

Servings: 8
Cooking Time: 4 To 5 Minutes
Ingredients:

- 340 g small, peeled, and deveined raw shrimp
- 85 g soft white cheese, room temperature
- 2 tablespoons natural yoghurt
- 1 teaspoon lemon juice
- 1 teaspoon dried dill weed, crushed
- Salt, to taste
- 4 small hothouse cucumbers, each approximately 6 inches long

Directions:
1. Pour 4 tablespoons water in bottom of air fryer drawer.
2. Place shrimp in air fryer basket in single layer and air fry at 200ºC for 4 to 5 minutes, just until done. Watch carefully because shrimp cooks quickly, and overcooking makes it tough.
3. Chop shrimp into small pieces, no larger than ½ inch. Refrigerate while mixing the remaining ingredients.
4. With a fork, mash and whip the soft white cheese until smooth.
5. Stir in the yoghurt and beat until smooth. Stir in lemon juice, dill weed, and chopped shrimp.
6. Taste for seasoning. If needed, add ¼ to ½ teaspoon salt to suit your taste.
7. Store in refrigerator until serving time.
8. When ready to serve, wash and dry cucumbers and split them lengthwise. Scoop out the seeds and turn cucumbers upside down on paper towels to drain for 10 minutes.
9. Just before filling, wipe centres of cucumbers dry. Spoon the shrimp mixture into the pirogues and cut in half crosswise. Serve immediately.

Avocado Fries

Servings: 8
Cooking Time: 10 Minutes
Ingredients:

- 60g plain flour
- Salt and ground black pepper, as required
- 2 eggs
- 1 teaspoon water
- 100g seasoned breadcrumbs
- 2 avocados, peeled, pitted and sliced into 8 pieces
- Non-stick cooking spray

Directions:
1. In a shallow bowl, mix together the flour, salt, and black pepper.
2. In a second bowl, add the egg and water and beat well.
3. In a third bowl, place the breadcrumbs.
4. Coat the avocado slices with flour mixture, then dip into egg mixture and finally, coat evenly with the breadcrumbs.
5. Now, spray the avocado slices with cooking spray evenly.
6. Grease one basket of Ninja Foodi 2-Basket Air Fryer.
7. Press either "Zone 1" and "Zone 2" and then rotate the knob to select "Air Fry".
8. Set the temperature to 200 degrees C and then set the time for 5 minutes to preheat.
9. After preheating, arrange the avocado slices into the basket.
10. Slide basket into Air Fryer and set the time for 10 minutes.
11. After cooking time is completed, remove the fries from Air Fryer and serve warm.

Tofu Veggie Meatballs

Servings: 4
Cooking Time: 10minutes
Ingredients:

- 122g firm tofu, drained
- 50g breadcrumbs
- 37g bamboo shoots, thinly sliced
- 22g carrots, shredded & steamed
- 1 tsp garlic powder
- 1 ½ tbsp soy sauce

- 2 tbsp cornstarch
- 3 dried shitake mushrooms, soaked & chopped
- Pepper
- Salt

Directions:
1. Add tofu and remaining ingredients into the food processor and process until well combined.
2. Insert a crisper plate in the Ninja Foodi air fryer baskets.
3. Make small balls from the tofu mixture and place them in both baskets.
4. Select zone 1, then select "air fry" mode and set the temperature to 380 degrees F for 10 minutes. Press "match" to match zone 2 settings to zone 1. Press "start/stop" to begin. Turn halfway through.

Nutrition:
- (Per serving) Calories 125 | Fat 1.8g |Sodium 614mg | Carbs 23.4g | Fiber 2.5g | Sugar 3.8g | Protein 5.3g

Ravioli

Servings: 2
Cooking Time: 6 Minutes

Ingredients:
- 12 frozen portions of ravioli
- ½ cup buttermilk
- ½ cup Italian breadcrumbs

Directions:
1. Place two bowls side by side. Put the buttermilk in one and breadcrumbs in the other.
2. Dip each piece of ravioli into the buttermilk then breadcrumbs, making sure to coat them as best as possible.
3. Place a crisper plate in both drawers. In each drawer, put four breaded ravioli pieces in a single layer. Insert the drawers into the unit.
4. Select zone 1, then AIR FRY, then set the temperature to 360 degrees F/ 180 degrees C with a 6-minute timer. To match zone 2 settings to zone 1, choose MATCH. To begin, select START/STOP.
5. Remove the ravioli from the drawers after the timer has finished.

Nutrition:
- (Per serving) Calories 481 | Fat 20g | Sodium 1162mg | Carbs 56g | Fiber 4g | Sugar 9g | Protein 19g

Cauliflower Cheese Patties

Servings: 4
Cooking Time: 10 Minutes

Ingredients:
- 2 eggs
- 200g cauliflower rice, microwave for 5 minutes
- 56g mozzarella cheese, shredded
- 22g parmesan cheese, grated
- 11g Mexican cheese, shredded
- ½ tsp onion powder
- 1 tsp dried basil
- 1 tsp garlic powder
- 33g breadcrumbs
- Pepper
- Salt

Directions:
1. Add cauliflower rice and remaining ingredients into the mixing bowl and mix until well combined.
2. Insert a crisper plate in the Ninja Foodi air fryer baskets.
3. Make patties from the cauliflower mixture and place them in both baskets.
4. Select zone 1, then select "air fry" mode and set the temperature to 390 degrees F for 10 minutes. Press "match" to match zone 2 settings to zone 1. Press "start/stop" to begin. Turn halfway through.

Nutrition:
- (Per serving) Calories 318 | Fat 18g |Sodium 951mg | Carbs 11.1g | Fiber 1.8g | Sugar 2.2g | Protein 25.6g

Lemony Pear Chips

Servings: 4
Cooking Time: 9 To 13 Minutes
Ingredients:
- 2 firm Bosc or Anjou pears, cut crosswise into ⅛-inch-thick slices
- 1 tablespoon freshly squeezed lemon juice
- ½ teaspoon ground cinnamon
- ⅛ teaspoon ground cardamom

Directions:
1. Preheat the air fryer to 190°C.
2. Separate the smaller stem-end pear rounds from the larger rounds with seeds. Remove the core and seeds from the larger slices. Sprinkle all slices with lemon juice, cinnamon, and cardamom.
3. Put the chips into the two air fryer baskets. Air fry for 5 to 8 minutes, or until light golden brown, shaking the baskets once during cooking. Remove from the air fryer.
4. Remove the chips from the air fryer. Cool and serve or store in an airtight container at room temperature up for to 2 days.

Mac And Cheese Balls

Servings: 4
Cooking Time: 20 Minutes
Ingredients:
- 1 cup panko breadcrumbs
- 4 cups prepared macaroni and cheese, refrigerated
- 3 tablespoons flour
- 1 teaspoon salt, divided
- 1 teaspoon ground black pepper, divided
- 1 teaspoon smoked paprika, divided
- ½ teaspoon garlic powder, divided
- 2 eggs
- 1 tablespoon milk
- ¼ cup ranch dressing, garlic aioli, or chipotle mayo, for dipping (optional)

Directions:
1. Preheat a conventional oven to 400 degrees F/ 200 degrees C.
2. Shake the breadcrumbs onto a baking sheet so that they're evenly distributed. Bake in the oven for 3 minutes, then shake and bake for an additional 1 to 2 minutes, or until toasted.
3. Form the chilled macaroni and cheese into golf ball-sized balls and set them aside.
4. Combine the flour, ½ teaspoon salt, ½ teaspoon black pepper, ½ teaspoon smoked paprika, and ¼ teaspoon garlic powder in a large mixing bowl.
5. In a small bowl, whisk together the eggs and milk.
6. Combine the breadcrumbs, remaining salt, pepper, paprika, and garlic powder in a mixing bowl.
7. To coat the macaroni and cheese balls, roll them in the flour mixture, then the egg mixture, and then the breadcrumb mixture.
8. Place a crisper plate in each drawer. Put the cheese balls in a single layer in each drawer. Insert the drawers into the unit.
9. Select zone 1, then AIR FRY, then set the temperature to 360 degrees F/ 180 degrees C with an 8-minute timer. To match zone 2 settings to zone 1, choose MATCH. To begin, select START/STOP.
10. Serve and enjoy!

Nutrition:
- (Per serving) Calories 489 | Fat 15.9g | Sodium 1402mg | Carbs 69.7g | Fiber 2.5g | Sugar 4g | Protein 16.9g

Air Fried Pot Stickers

Servings: 30 Pot Stickers
Cooking Time: 18 To 20 Minutes
Ingredients:
- 120 ml finely chopped cabbage
- 60 ml finely chopped red pepper
- 2 spring onions, finely chopped
- 1 egg, beaten
- 2 tablespoons cocktail sauce
- 2 teaspoons low-salt soy sauce
- 30 wonton wrappers
- 1 tablespoon water, for brushing the wrappers

Directions:
1. Preheat the air fryer to 180°C.
2. In a small bowl, combine the cabbage, pepper, spring onions, egg, cocktail sauce, and soy sauce, and mix well.
3. Put about 1 teaspoon of the mixture in the centre of each wonton wrapper. Fold the wrapper in half, covering the filling; dampen the edges with water, and seal. You can crimp the edges of the wrapper with your fingers, so they look like the pot stickers you get in restaurants. Brush them with water.
4. Place the pot stickers in the two air fryer baskets and air fry for 9 to 10 minutes, or until the pot stickers are hot and the bottoms are lightly browned.
5. Serve hot.

Crab Rangoon Dip With Crispy Wonton Strips

Servings: 6
Cooking Time: 15 Minutes
Ingredients:
- FOR THE DIP
- 1 (6-ounce) can pink crab, drained
- 8 ounces (16 tablespoons) cream cheese, at room temperature
- ½ cup sour cream
- 1 tablespoon chopped scallions
- ½ teaspoon garlic powder
- 1 teaspoon Worcestershire sauce
- ¼ teaspoon kosher salt
- 1 cup shredded part-skim mozzarella cheese
- FOR THE WONTON STRIPS
- 12 wonton wrappers
- 1 tablespoon olive oil
- ¼ teaspoon kosher salt

Directions:
1. To prep the dip: In a medium bowl, mix the crab, cream cheese, sour cream, scallions, garlic powder, Worcestershire sauce, and salt until smooth.
2. To prep the wonton strips: Brush both sides of the wonton wrappers with the oil and sprinkle with salt. Cut the wonton wrappers into ¾-inch-wide strips.
3. To cook the dip and strips: Pour the dip into the Zone 1 basket, top with the mozzarella cheese, and insert the basket in the unit. Install a crisper plate in the Zone 2 basket, add the wonton strips, and insert the basket in the unit.
4. Select Zone 1, select BAKE, set the temperature to 330°F, and set the time to 15 minutes.
5. Select Zone 2, select AIR FRY, set the temperature to 350°F, and set the time to 6 minutes. Select SMART FINISH.
6. Press START/PAUSE to begin cooking.
7. When the Zone 2 timer reads 4 minutes, press START/PAUSE. Remove the basket and shake well to redistribute the wonton strips. Reinsert the basket and press START/PAUSE to resume cooking.
8. When the Zone 2 timer reads 2 minutes, press START/PAUSE. Remove the basket and shake well to redistribute the wonton strips. Reinsert the basket and press START/PAUSE to resume cooking.
9. When cooking is complete, the dip will be bubbling and golden brown on top and the wonton strips will be crunchy. Serve warm.

Nutrition:
- (Per serving) Calories: 315; Total fat: 23g; Saturated fat: 12g; Carbohydrates: 14g; Fiber: 0.5g; Protein: 14g; Sodium: 580mg

Chicken Stuffed Mushrooms

Servings: 6
Cooking Time: 15 Minutes.

Ingredients:
- 6 large fresh mushrooms, stems removed
- Stuffing:
- ½ cup chicken meat, cubed
- 1 (4 ounces) package cream cheese, softened
- ¼ lb. imitation crabmeat, flaked
- 1 cup butter
- 1 garlic clove, peeled and minced
- Black pepper and salt to taste
- Garlic powder to taste
- Crushed red pepper to taste

Directions:
1. Melt and heat butter in a skillet over medium heat.
2. Add chicken and sauté for 5 minutes.
3. Add in all the remaining ingredients for the stuffing.
4. Cook for 5 minutes, then turn off the heat.
5. Allow the mixture to cool. Stuff each mushroom with a tablespoon of this mixture.
6. Divide the stuffed mushrooms in the two crisper plates.
7. Return the crisper plate to the Ninja Foodi Dual Zone Air Fryer.
8. Choose the Air Fry mode for Zone 1 and set the temperature to 375 degrees F and the time to 15 minutes.
9. Select the "MATCH" button to copy the settings for Zone 2.
10. Initiate cooking by pressing the START/STOP button.
11. Serve warm.

Nutrition:
- (Per serving) Calories 180 | Fat 3.2g |Sodium 133mg | Carbs 32g | Fiber 1.1g | Sugar 1.8g | Protein 9g

Waffle Fries

Servings: 2
Cooking Time: 15 Minutes

Ingredients:
- 2 russet potatoes
- ½ teaspoon seasoning salt

Directions:
1. If desired, peel the potatoes.
2. With Wave-Waffle Cutter, slice potatoes by turning them one-quarter turn after each pass over the blade.
3. In a mixing dish, toss the potato pieces with the seasoning salt. Toss the potatoes in the seasoning to ensure that it is uniformly distributed.
4. Place a baking sheet on the baskets.
5. Press either "Zone 1" or "Zone 2" and then rotate the knob to select "Air Fryer".
6. Set the temperature to 200 degrees C, and then set the time for 5 minutes to preheat.
7. After preheating, arrange them into the basket.
8. Slide the basket into the Air Fryer and set the time for 15 minutes.
9. After cooking time is completed, place on a wire rack for a few minutes, then transfer onto serving plates and serve.

Chapter 4: Breakfast Recipes

Breakfast Pitta

Servings: 2
Cooking Time: 6 Minutes
Ingredients:
- 1 wholemeal pitta
- 2 teaspoons olive oil
- ½ shallot, diced
- ¼ teaspoon garlic, minced
- 1 large egg
- ¼ teaspoon dried oregano
- ¼ teaspoon dried thyme
- ⅛ teaspoon salt
- 2 tablespoons shredded Parmesan cheese

Directions:
1. Brush the top of the pitta with olive oil, then spread the diced shallot and minced garlic over the pitta. Crack the egg into a small bowl or ramekin, and season it with oregano, thyme, and salt.
2. Place the pitta into the zone 1 drawer, and gently pour the egg onto the top of the pitta. Sprinkle with cheese over the top.
3. Select Bake button and adjust temperature to 190°C, set time to 6 minutes and press Start. After the end, allow to cool for 5 minutes before cutting into pieces for serving.

Egg And Bacon Muffins

Servings: 1
Cooking Time: 15 Minutes
Ingredients:
- 2 eggs
- Salt and ground black pepper, to taste
- 1 tablespoon green pesto
- 85 g shredded Cheddar cheese
- 140 g cooked bacon
- 1 spring onion, chopped

Directions:
1. Line a cupcake tin with parchment paper. Beat the eggs with pepper, salt, and pesto in a bowl. Mix in the cheese.
2. Pour the eggs into the cupcake tin and top with the bacon and spring onion.
3. Place the cupcake tin into the zone 1 drawer and bake at 180°C for 15 minutes, or until the egg is set. Serve immediately.

Baked Peach Oatmeal

Servings: 6
Cooking Time: 30 Minutes
Ingredients:
- Olive oil cooking spray
- 475 ml certified gluten-free rolled oats
- 475 ml unsweetened almond milk
- 60 ml honey, plus more for drizzling (optional)
- 120 ml non-fat plain Greek yoghurt
- 1 teaspoon vanilla extract
- ½ teaspoon ground cinnamon
- ¼ teaspoon salt
- 350 ml diced peaches, divided, plus more for serving (optional)

Directions:
1. Lightly coat the inside of a 6-inch cake pan with olive oil cooking spray. In a large bowl, mix together the oats, almond milk, honey, yoghurt, vanilla, cinnamon, and salt until well combined.
2. Fold in 180 ml peaches and then pour the mixture into the prepared cake pan. Sprinkle the remaining peaches across the top of the oatmeal mixture.
3. Place the cake pan into the zone 1 drawer and bake at 190°C for 30 minutes. Allow to set and cool for 5 minutes before serving with additional fresh fruit and honey for drizzling, if desired.

Buttermilk Biscuits With Roasted Stone Fruit Compote

Servings: 4
Cooking Time: 20 Minutes
Ingredients:
- FOR THE BISCUITS
- 1⅓ cups all-purpose flour
- 2 teaspoons sugar
- 2 teaspoons baking powder
- ½ teaspoon baking soda
- ½ teaspoon kosher salt
- 4 tablespoons (½ stick) very cold unsalted butter
- ½ cup plus 1 tablespoon low-fat buttermilk
- FOR THE FRUIT COMPOTE
- 2 peaches, peeled and diced
- 2 plums, peeled and diced
- ¼ cup water
- 2 teaspoons honey
- ⅛ teaspoon ground ginger (optional)

Directions:
1. To prep the biscuits: In a small bowl, combine the flour, sugar, baking powder, baking soda, and salt. Using the large holes on a box grater, grate in the butter. Stir in the buttermilk to form a thick dough.
2. Place the dough on a lightly floured surface and gently pat it into a ½-inch-thick disc. Fold the dough in half, then rotate the whole thing 90 degrees, pat into a ½-inch thick disc and fold again. Repeat until you have folded the dough four times.
3. Pat the dough out a final time into a ½-inch-thick disc and use a 3-inch biscuit cutter to cut 4 biscuits from the dough (discard the scraps).
4. To prep the fruit compote: In a large bowl, stir together the peaches, plums, water, honey, and ginger (if using).
5. To cook the biscuits and compote: Install a crisper plate in the Zone 1 basket, place the biscuits in the basket, and insert the basket in the unit. Place the fruit in the Zone 2 basket and insert the basket in the unit.
6. Select Zone 1, select AIR FRY, set the temperature to 400°F, and set the time to 10 minutes.
7. Select Zone 2, select ROAST, set the temperature to 350°F, and set the time to 20 minutes. Select SMART FINISH.
8. Press START/PAUSE to begin cooking.
9. When the Zone 2 timer reads 10 minutes, press START/PAUSE. Remove the basket and stir the compote. Reinsert the basket and press START/PAUSE to resume cooking.
10. When cooking is complete, the biscuits will be golden brown and crisp on top and the fruit will be soft. Transfer the biscuits to a plate to cool. Lightly mash the fruit to form a thick, jammy sauce.
11. Split the biscuits in half horizontally and serve topped with fruit compote.

Nutrition:
- (Per serving) Calories: 332; Total fat: 12g; Saturated fat: 7.5g; Carbohydrates: 50g; Fiber: 2.5g; Protein: 6g; Sodium: 350mg

Baked Mushroom And Mozzarella Frittata With Breakfast Potatoes

Servings: 4
Cooking Time: 35 Minutes
Ingredients:
- FOR THE FRITTATA
- 8 large eggs
- ⅓ cup whole milk
- 1 teaspoon kosher salt
- ½ teaspoon freshly ground black pepper
- 1 cup sliced cremini mushrooms (about 2 ounces)
- 1 teaspoon olive oil
- 2 ounces part-skim mozzarella cheese, cut into ½-inch cubes
- FOR THE POTATOES
- 2 russet potatoes, cut into ½-inch cubes
- 1 tablespoon olive oil
- ½ teaspoon garlic powder
- ¼ teaspoon kosher salt
- ¼ teaspoon freshly ground black pepper

Directions:
1. To prep the frittata: In a large bowl, whisk together the eggs, milk, salt, and pepper. Stir in the mushrooms.
2. To prep the potatoes: In a large bowl, combine the potatoes, olive oil, garlic powder, salt, and black pepper.

3. To cook the frittata and potatoes: Brush the bottom of the Zone 1 basket with 1 teaspoon of olive oil. Add the egg mixture to the basket, top with the mozzarella cubes, and insert the basket in the unit. Install a crisper plate in the Zone 2 basket. Place the potatoes in the basket and insert the basket in the unit.
4. Select Zone 1, select BAKE, set the temperature to 350°F, and set the time to 30 minutes.
5. Select Zone 2, select AIR FRY, set the temperature to 400°F, and set the time to 35 minutes. Select SMART FINISH.
6. Press START/PAUSE to begin cooking.
7. When the Zone 2 timer reads 15 minutes, press START/PAUSE. Remove the basket and shake the potatoes for 10 seconds. Reinsert the basket and press START/PAUSE to resume cooking.
8. When cooking is complete, the frittata will pull away from the edges of the basket and the potatoes will be golden brown. Transfer the frittata to a cutting board and cut into 4 portions. Serve with the potatoes.

Nutrition:
- (Per serving) Calories: 307; Total fat: 17g; Saturated fat: 5.5g; Carbohydrates: 18g; Fiber: 1g; Protein: 19g; Sodium: 600mg

Bacon, Cheese, And Avocado Melt & Cheesy Scrambled Eggs

Servings: 4
Cooking Time: 9 Minutes
Ingredients:

- Bacon, Cheese, and Avocado Melt:
- 1 avocado
- 4 slices cooked bacon, chopped
- 2 tablespoons salsa
- 1 tablespoon double cream
- 60 ml shredded Cheddar cheese

- Cheesy Scrambled Eggs:
- 1 teaspoon unsalted butter
- 2 large eggs
- 2 tablespoons milk
- 2 tablespoons shredded Cheddar cheese
- Salt and freshly ground black pepper, to taste

Directions:
1. Make the Bacon, Cheese, and Avocado Melt :
2. Preheat the zone 1 air fryer drawer to 204ºC.
3. Slice the avocado in half lengthwise and remove the stone. To ensure the avocado halves do not roll in the drawer, slice a thin piece of skin off the base.
4. In a small bowl, combine the bacon, salsa, and cream. Divide the mixture between the avocado halves and top with the cheese.
5. Place the avocado halves in the zone 1 air fryer drawer and air fry for 3 to 5 minutes until the cheese has melted and begins to brown. Serve warm.
6. Make the Cheesy Scrambled Eggs :
7. Preheat the zone 2 air fryer drawer to 150ºC. Place the butter in a baking pan and cook for 1 to 2 minutes, until melted.
8. In a small bowl, whisk together the eggs, milk, and cheese. Season with salt and black pepper. Transfer the mixture to the pan.
9. Cook for 3 minutes. Stir the eggs and push them toward the center of the pan.
10. Cook for another 2 minutes, then stir again. Cook for another 2 minutes, until the eggs are just cooked. Serve warm.

Bacon And Spinach Egg Muffins

Servings: 6
Cooking Time: 12 To 14 Minutes
Ingredients:

- 6 large eggs
- 60 ml double (whipping) cream
- ½ teaspoon sea salt
- ¼ teaspoon freshly ground black pepper

- ¼ teaspoon cayenne pepper (optional)
- 180 ml frozen chopped spinach, thawed and drained
- 4 strips cooked bacon, crumbled
- 60 g shredded Cheddar cheese

Directions:

1. In a large bowl, whisk together the eggs, double cream, salt, black pepper, and cayenne pepper.
2. Divide the spinach and bacon among 6 silicone muffin cups. Place the muffin cups in the zone 1 air fryer drawer.
3. Divide the egg mixture among the muffin cups. Top with the cheese.
4. Set the temperature to 150ºC. Bake for 12 to 14 minutes, until the eggs are set and cooked through.

Eggs In Avocado Cups

Servings: 4
Cooking Time: 12 Minutes
Ingredients:

- 2 avocados, halved and pitted
- 4 eggs
- Salt and ground black pepper, as required

Directions:
1. Line either basket of "Zone 1" and "Zone 2" of Ninja Foodi 2-Basket Air Fryer with a greased square piece of foil.
2. Press your chosen zone - "Zone 1" and "Zone 2" and then rotate the knob to select "Bake".
3. Set the temperature to 200 degrees C and then set the time for 5 minutes to preheat.
4. Meanwhile, carefully scoop out about 2 teaspoons of flesh from each avocado half.
5. Crack 1 egg in each avocado half and sprinkle with salt and black pepper.
6. After preheating, arrange 2 avocado halves into the basket.
7. Slide the basket into the Air Fryer and set the time for 12 minutes.
8. After cooking time is completed, transfer the avocado halves and onto serving plates and serve hot.

Potatoes Lyonnaise

Servings: 4
Cooking Time: 31 Minutes
Ingredients:

- 1 sweet/mild onion, sliced
- 1 teaspoon butter, melted
- 1 teaspoon brown sugar
- 2 large white potatoes (about 450 g in total), sliced ½-inch thick
- 1 tablespoon vegetable oil
- Salt and freshly ground black pepper, to taste

Directions:
1. Preheat the air fryer to 188ºC.
2. Toss the sliced onions, melted butter and brown sugar together in the zone 1 air fryer drawer. Air fry for 8 minutes, shaking the drawer occasionally to help the onions cook evenly.
3. While the onions are cooking, bring a saucepan of salted water to a boil on the stovetop. Par-cook the potatoes in boiling water for 3 minutes. Drain the potatoes and pat them dry with a clean kitchen towel.
4. Add the potatoes to the onions in the zone 1 air fryer drawer and drizzle with vegetable oil. Toss to coat the potatoes with the oil and season with salt and freshly ground black pepper.
5. Increase the air fryer temperature to 204ºC and air fry for 20 minutes, tossing the vegetables a few times during the cooking time to help the potatoes brown evenly.
6. Season with salt and freshly ground black pepper and serve warm.

Donuts

Servings: 6
Cooking Time: 15 Minutes
Ingredients:

- 1 cup granulated sugar
- 2 tablespoons ground cinnamon
- 1 can refrigerated flaky buttermilk biscuits
- ¼ cup unsalted butter, melted

Directions:
1. Combine the sugar and cinnamon in a small shallow bowl and set aside.
2. Remove the biscuits from the can and put them on a chopping board, separated. Cut holes in the center of each biscuit with a 1-inch round biscuit cutter (or a similarly sized bottle cap).

3. Place a crisper plate in each drawer. In each drawer, place 4 biscuits in a single layer. Insert the drawers into the unit.
4. Select zone 1, then AIR FRY, then set the temperature to 360 degrees F/ 180 degrees C with a 10-minute timer. To match zone 2 settings to zone 1, choose MATCH. To begin cooking, select START/STOP.
5. Remove the donuts from the drawers after the timer has finished.

Nutrition:
- (Per serving) Calories 223 | Fat 8g | Sodium 150mg | Carbs 40g | Fiber 1.4g | Sugar 34.2g | Protein 0.8g

Air Fried Bacon And Eggs

Servings: 1
Cooking Time: 10 Minutes
Ingredients:
- 2 eggs
- 2 slices bacon

Directions:
1. Grease a ramekin using cooking spray.
2. Install the crisper plate in the zone 1 drawer and place the bacon inside it. Insert the drawer into the unit.
3. Crack the eggs and add them to the greased ramekin.
4. Install the crisper plate in the zone 2 drawer and place the ramekin inside it. Insert the drawer into the unit.
5. Select zone 1 to AIR FRY for 9–11 minutes at 400 degrees F/ 200 degrees C. Select zone 2 to AIR FRY for 8–9 minutes at 350 degrees F/ 175 degrees C. Press SYNC.
6. Press START/STOP to begin cooking.
7. Enjoy!

Nutrition:
- (Per serving) Calories 331 | Fat 24.5g | Sodium 1001mg | Carbs 1.2g | Fiber 0g | Sugar 0.7g | Protein 25.3g

Perfect Cinnamon Toast

Servings: 6
Cooking Time: 10 Minutes
Ingredients:
- 12 slices whole-wheat bread
- 1 stick butter, room temperature
- ½ cup white sugar
- 1½ teaspoons ground cinnamon
- 1½ teaspoons pure vanilla extract
- 1 pinch kosher salt
- 2 pinches freshly ground black pepper (optional)

Directions:
1. Mash the softened butter with a fork or the back of a spoon in a bowl. Add the sugar, cinnamon, vanilla, and salt. Stir until everything is well combined.
2. Spread one-sixth of the mixture onto each slice of bread, making sure to cover the entire surface.
3. Install a crisper plate in both drawers. Place half the bread sliced in the zone 1 drawer and half in the zone 2 drawer, then insert the drawers into the unit.
4. Select zone 1, select AIR FRY, set temperature to 400 degrees F/ 200 degrees C, and set time to 5 minutes. Select MATCH to match zone 2 settings to zone 1. Press theSTART/STOP button to begin cooking
5. When cooking is complete, remove the slices and cut them diagonally.
6. Serve immediately.

Nutrition:
- (Per serving) Calories 322 | Fat 16.5g | Sodium 249mg | Carbs 39.3g | Fiber 4.2g | Sugar 18.2g | Protein 8.2g

Parmesan Sausage Egg Muffins

Servings: 4
Cooking Time: 20 Minutes
Ingredients:
- 170 g Italian-seasoned sausage, sliced
- 6 eggs
- 30 ml double cream
- Salt and ground black pepper, to taste
- 85 g Parmesan cheese, grated

Directions:
1. Preheat the air fryer to 176°C. Grease a muffin pan.
2. Put the sliced sausage in the muffin pan.
3. Beat the eggs with the cream in a bowl and season with salt and pepper.
4. Pour half of the mixture over the sausages in the pan.
5. Sprinkle with cheese and the remaining egg mixture.
6. Bake in the preheated air fryer for 20 minutes or until set.
7. Serve immediately.

Crispy Hash Browns

Servings: 4
Cooking Time: 13 Minutes.
Ingredients:
- 3 russet potatoes
- ¼ cup chopped green peppers
- ¼ cup chopped red peppers
- ¼ cup chopped onions
- 2 garlic cloves chopped
- 1 teaspoon paprika
- Salt and black pepper, to taste
- 2 teaspoons olive oil

Directions:
1. Peel and grate all the potatoes with the help of a cheese grater.
2. Add potato shreds to a bowl filled with cold water and leave it soaked for 25 minutes.
3. Drain the water and place the potato shreds on a plate lined with a paper towel.
4. Transfer the shreds to a dry bowl and add olive oil, paprika, garlic, and black pepper.
5. Make four flat patties out of the potato mixture and place two into each of the crisper plate.
6. Return the crisper plate to the Ninja Foodi Dual Zone Air Fryer.
7. Choose the Air Fry mode for Zone 1 and set the temperature to 390 degrees F and set the time to 13 minutes.
8. Select the "MATCH" button to copy the settings for Zone 2.
9. Initiate cooking by pressing the START/STOP button.
10. Flip the potato hash browns once cooked halfway through, then resume cooking.
11. Once done, serve warm.

Nutrition:
- (Per serving) Calories 190 | Fat 18g | Sodium 150mg | Carbs 0.6g | Fiber 0.4g | Sugar 0.4g | Protein 7.2g

Cajun Breakfast Sausage

Servings: 8
Cooking Time: 15 To 20 Minutes
Ingredients:
- 680 g 85% lean turkey mince
- 3 cloves garlic, finely chopped
- ¼ onion, grated
- 1 teaspoon Tabasco sauce
- 1 teaspoon Cajun seasoning
- 1 teaspoon dried thyme
- ½ teaspoon paprika
- ½ teaspoon cayenne

Directions:
1. Preheat the air fryer to 188°C.

2. In a large bowl, combine the turkey, garlic, onion, Tabasco, Cajun seasoning, thyme, paprika, and cayenne. Mix with clean hands until thoroughly combined. Shape into 16 patties, about ½ inch thick.
3. Arrange the patties in a single layer in the two air fryer drawers. Pausing halfway through the cooking time to flip the patties, air fry for 15 to 20 minutes until a thermometer inserted into the thickest portion registers 74ºC.

Baked Egg And Mushroom Cups

Servings: 6
Cooking Time: 15 Minutes
Ingredients:
- Olive oil cooking spray
- 6 large eggs
- 1 garlic clove, minced
- ½ teaspoon salt
- ½ teaspoon black pepper
- Pinch red pepper flakes
- 230 g baby mushrooms, sliced
- 235 ml fresh baby spinach
- 2 spring onions, white parts and green parts, diced

Directions:
1. Lightly coat the inside of six silicone muffin cups or a six-cup muffin tin with olive oil cooking spray. In a large bowl, beat the eggs, garlic, salt, pepper, and red pepper flakes for 1 to 2 minutes, or until well combined.
2. Fold in the mushrooms, spinach, and spring onions. Divide the mixture evenly among the muffin cups. Place into the zone 1 drawer.
3. Select Bake button and adjust temperature to 160ºC, set time to 12 to 15 minutes and press Start. Remove after the end and allow to cool for 5 minutes before serving.

Buffalo Chicken Breakfast Muffins

Servings: 10
Cooking Time: 13 To 16 Minutes
Ingredients:
- 170 g shredded cooked chicken
- 85 g blue cheese, crumbled
- 2 tablespoons unsalted butter, melted
- 80 ml Buffalo hot sauce, such as Frank's RedHot
- 1 teaspoon minced garlic
- 6 large eggs
- Sea salt and freshly ground black pepper, to taste
- Avocado oil spray

Directions:
1. In a large bowl, stir together the chicken, blue cheese, melted butter, hot sauce, and garlic.
2. In a medium bowl or large liquid measuring cup, beat the eggs. Season with salt and pepper.
3. Spray 10 silicone muffin cups with oil. Divide the chicken mixture among the cups, and pour the egg mixture over top.
4. Place the cups in the two air fryer baskets and set to 150ºC. Bake for 13 to 16 minutes, until the muffins are set and cooked through.

Breakfast Stuffed Peppers

Servings: 4
Cooking Time: 13 Minutes
Ingredients:
- 2 capsicums, halved, seeds removed
- 4 eggs
- 1 teaspoon olive oil
- 1 pinch salt and pepper
- 1 pinch sriracha flakes

Directions:
1. Cut each capsicum in half and place two halves in each air fryer basket.
2. Crack one egg into each capsicum and top it with black pepper, salt, sriracha flakes and olive oil.
3. Return the air fryer basket 1 to Zone 1, and basket 2 to Zone 2 of the Ninja Foodi 2-Basket Air Fryer.
4. Choose the "Air Fry" mode for Zone 1 at 390 degrees F and 13 minutes of cooking time.
5. Select the "MATCH COOK" option to copy the settings for Zone 2.

6. Initiate cooking by pressing the START/PAUSE BUTTON.
7. Serve warm.

Nutrition:
- (Per serving) Calories 237 | Fat 19g | Sodium 518mg | Carbs 7g | Fiber 1.5g | Sugar 3.4g | Protein 12g

Easy Pancake Doughnuts

Servings: 8
Cooking Time: 9 Minutes

Ingredients:
- 2 eggs
- 50g sugar
- 125ml vegetable oil
- 240g pancake mix
- 1 ½ tbsp cinnamon

Directions:
1. In a bowl, mix pancake mix, eggs, cinnamon, sugar, and oil until well combined.
2. Pour the doughnut mixture into the silicone doughnut moulds.
3. Insert a crisper plate in Ninja Foodi air fryer baskets.
4. Place doughnut moulds in both baskets.
5. Select zone 1 then select "air fry" mode and set the temperature to 355 degrees F for 9 minutes. Press "match" to match zone 2 settings to zone 1. Press "start/stop" to begin.

Nutrition:
- (Per serving) Calories 163 | Fat 14.7g | Sodium 16mg | Carbs 7.4g | Fiber 0.7g | Sugar 6.4g | Protein 1.4g

French Toasts

Servings: 4
Cooking Time: 6 Minutes

Ingredients:
- 4 eggs
- 120g evaporated milk
- 6 tablespoons sugar
- 4 teaspoons olive oil
- ¼ teaspoon ground cinnamon
- ¼ teaspoon vanilla extract
- 8 bread slices

Directions:
1. Line each basket of "Zone 1" and "Zone 2" with a greased piece of foil.
2. Then Press your chosen zone - "Zone 1" or "Zone 2" and then rotate the knob to select "Air Fry".
3. Set the temperature to 200 degrees C and then set the time for 5 minutes to preheat.
4. In a large bowl, add all ingredients except for bread slices and beat until well combined.
5. Coat the bread slices with egg mixture evenly.
6. After preheating, arrange 4 bread slices into the basket of each zone.
7. Slide the basket into the Air Fryer and set the time for 6 minutes.
8. While cooking, flip the slices once halfway through.
9. After cooking time is completed, remove the French toasts from Air Fryer and serve warm.

Cheesy Baked Eggs

Servings: 4
Cooking Time: 16 Minutes

Ingredients:
- 4 large eggs
- 57g smoked gouda, shredded
- Everything bagel seasoning, to taste
- Salt and pepper to taste

Directions:
1. Crack one egg in each ramekin.
2. Top the egg with bagel seasoning, black pepper, salt and gouda.
3. Place 2 ramekins in each air fryer basket.

4. Return the air fryer basket 1 to Zone 1, and basket 2 to Zone 2 of the Ninja Foodi 2-Basket Air Fryer.
5. Choose the "Air Fry" mode for Zone 1 and set the temperature to 400 degrees F and 16 minutes of cooking time.
6. Select the "MATCH COOK" option to copy the settings for Zone 2.
7. Initiate cooking by pressing the START/PAUSE BUTTON.
8. Serve warm.

Nutrition:
- (Per serving) Calories 190 | Fat 18g |Sodium 150mg | Carbs 0.6g | Fiber 0.4g | Sugar 0.4g | Protein 7.2g

Parmesan Ranch Risotto And Oat And Chia Porridge

Servings: 6
Cooking Time: 30 Minutes

Ingredients:
- Parmesan Ranch Risotto:
- 1 tablespoon olive oil
- 1 clove garlic, minced
- 1 tablespoon unsalted butter
- 1 onion, diced
- 180 ml Arborio rice
- 475 ml chicken stock, boiling
- 120 ml Parmesan cheese, grated
- Oat and Chia Porridge:
- 2 tablespoons peanut butter
- 4 tablespoons honey
- 1 tablespoon butter, melted
- 1 L milk
- 475 ml oats
- 235 ml chia seeds

Directions:
1. Make the Parmesan Ranch Risotto :
2. Preheat the air fryer to 200ºC.
3. Grease a round baking tin with olive oil and stir in the garlic, butter, and onion.
4. Transfer the tin to the zone 1 air fryer basket and bake for 4 minutes. Add the rice and bake for 4 more minutes.
5. Turn the air fryer to 160ºC and pour in the chicken stock. Cover and bake for 22 minutes.
6. Scatter with cheese and serve.
7. Make the Oat and Chia Porridge :
8. Preheat the air fryer to 200ºC.
9. Put the peanut butter, honey, butter, and milk in a bowl and stir to mix. Add the oats and chia seeds and stir.
10. Transfer the mixture to a bowl and bake in the zone 2 air fryer basket for 5 minutes. Give another stir before serving.

Blueberry Coffee Cake And Maple Sausage Patties

Servings:6
Cooking Time: 25 Minutes

Ingredients:
- FOR THE COFFEE CAKE
- 6 tablespoons unsalted butter, at room temperature, divided
- ⅓ cup granulated sugar
- 1 large egg
- 1 teaspoon vanilla extract
- ¼ cup whole milk
- 1½ cups all-purpose flour, divided
- 1 teaspoon baking powder
- ¼ teaspoon salt
- 1 cup blueberries
- ¼ cup packed light brown sugar
- ½ teaspoon ground cinnamon
- FOR THE SAUSAGE PATTIES
- ½ pound ground pork
- 2 tablespoons maple syrup
- ½ teaspoon dried sage
- ½ teaspoon dried thyme
- 1½ teaspoons kosher salt
- ½ teaspoon crushed fennel seeds
- ½ teaspoon red pepper flakes (optional)
- ¼ teaspoon freshly ground black pepper

Directions:

1. To prep the coffee cake: In a large bowl, cream together 4 tablespoons of butter with the granulated sugar. Beat in the egg, vanilla, and milk.
2. Stir in 1 cup of flour, along with the baking soda and salt, to form a thick batter. Fold in the blueberries.
3. In a second bowl, mix the remaining 2 tablespoons of butter, remaining ½ cup of flour, the brown sugar, and cinnamon to form a dry crumbly mixture.
4. To prep the sausage patties: In a large bowl, mix the pork, maple syrup, sage, thyme, salt, fennel seeds, red pepper flakes (if using), and black pepper until just combined.
5. Divide the mixture into 6 equal patties about ½ inch thick.
6. To cook the coffee cake and sausage patties: Spread the cake batter into the Zone 1 basket, top with the crumble mixture, and insert the basket in the unit. Install a crisper plate in the Zone 2 basket, add the sausage patties in a single layer, and insert the basket in the unit.
7. Select Zone 1, select BAKE, set the temperature to 350°F, and set the time to 25 minutes.
8. Select Zone 2, select AIR FRY, set the temperature to 375°F, and set the time to 12 minutes. Select SMART FINISH.
9. Press START/PAUSE to begin cooking.
10. When the Zone 2 timer reads 6 minutes, press START/PAUSE. Remove the basket and use silicone-tipped tongs to flip the sausage patties. Reinsert the basket and press START/PAUSE to resume cooking.
11. When cooking is complete, let the coffee cake cool for at least 5 minutes, then cut into 6 slices. Serve warm or at room temperature with the sausage patties.

Nutrition:
- (Per serving) Calories: 395; Total fat: 15g; Saturated fat: 8g; Carbohydrates: 53g; Fiber: 1.5g; Protein: 14g; Sodium: 187mg

Cinnamon Toast

Servings: 6
Cooking Time: 5 Minutes
Ingredients:
- 12 slices bread
- 115g butter, at room temperature
- 100g white sugar
- 1½ teaspoons ground cinnamon
- 1½ teaspoons pure vanilla extract
- 1 pinch of salt

Directions:
1. Softened butter is mashed with a fork or the back of a spoon, and then sugar, cinnamon, vanilla, and salt are added.
2. Stir everything together thoroughly.
3. Spread one-sixth of the mixture onto each slice of bread, covering the entire surface.
4. Press your chosen zone - "Zone 1" or "Zone 2" and then rotate the knob to select "Air Fryer".
5. Set the temperature to 200 degrees C, and then set the time for 3 minutes to preheat.
6. After preheating, arrange bread into the basket of each zone.
7. Slide the basket into the Air Fryer and set the time for 5 minutes.
8. After cooking time is completed, remove both baskets from Air Fryer.
9. Cut bread slices diagonally and serve.

Broccoli-mushroom Frittata And Chimichanga Breakfast Burrito

Servings: 4
Cooking Time: 20 Minutes
Ingredients:
- Broccoli-Mushroom Frittata:
- 1 tablespoon olive oil
- 350 ml broccoli florets, finely chopped
- 120 ml sliced brown mushrooms
- 60 ml finely chopped onion
- ½ teaspoon salt
- ¼ teaspoon freshly ground black pepper
- 6 eggs
- 60 ml Parmesan cheese
- Chimichanga Breakfast Burrito:
- 2 large (10- to 12-inch) flour tortillas

- 120 ml canned refried beans (pinto or black work equally well)
- 4 large eggs, cooked scrambled
- 4 corn tortilla chips, crushed
- 120 ml grated chili cheese
- 12 pickled jalapeño slices
- 1 tablespoon vegetable oil
- Guacamole, salsa, and sour cream, for serving (optional)

Directions:

1. Make the Broccoli-Mushroom Frittata :
2. In a nonstick cake pan, combine the olive oil, broccoli, mushrooms, onion, salt, and pepper. Stir until the vegetables are thoroughly coated with oil. Place the cake pan in the zone 1 air fryer basket and set the air fryer to 205°C. Air fry for 5 minutes until the vegetables soften.
3. Meanwhile, in a medium bowl, whisk the eggs and Parmesan until thoroughly combined. Pour the egg mixture into the pan and shake gently to distribute the vegetables. Air fry for another 15 minutes until the eggs are set.
4. Remove from the air fryer and let sit for 5 minutes to cool slightly. Use a silicone spatula to gently lift the frittata onto a plate before serving.
5. Make the Chimichanga Breakfast Burrito :
6. Place the tortillas on a work surface and divide the refried beans between them, spreading them in a rough rectangle in the center of the tortillas. Top the beans with the scrambled eggs, crushed chips, cheese, and jalapeños. Fold one side over the fillings, then fold in each short side and roll up the rest of the way like a burrito.
7. Brush the outside of the burritos with the oil, then transfer to the zone 2 air fryer basket, seam-side down. Air fry at 175°C until the tortillas are browned and crisp and the filling is warm throughout, about 10 minutes.
8. Transfer the chimichangas to plates and serve warm with guacamole, salsa, and sour cream, if you like.

Chapter 5: Vegetables And Sides Recipes

Brussels Sprouts

Servings: 2
Cooking Time: 20
Ingredients:
- 2 pounds Brussels sprouts
- 2 tablespoons avocado oil
- Salt and pepper, to taste
- 1 cup pine nuts, roasted

Directions:
1. Trim the bottom of Brussels sprouts.
2. Take a bowl and combine the avocado oil, salt, and black pepper.
3. Toss the Brussels sprouts well.
4. Divide it in both air fryer baskets.
5. For the zone 1 basket use AIR fry mode for 20 minutes at 390 degrees F.
6. Select the MATCH button for the zone 2 basket.
7. Once the Brussels sprouts get crisp and tender, take out and serve.

Nutrition:
- (Per serving) Calories 672| Fat 50g| Sodium 115mg | Carbs 51g | Fiber 20.2g | Sugar 12.3g | Protein 25g

Acorn Squash Slices

Servings: 6
Cooking Time: 10 Minutes
Ingredients:
- 2 medium acorn squashes
- ⅔ cup packed brown sugar
- ½ cup butter, melted

Directions:
1. Cut the squash in half, remove the seeds and slice into ½ inch slices.
2. Place the squash slices in the air fryer baskets.
3. Drizzle brown sugar and butter over the squash slices.
4. Return the air fryer basket 1 to Zone 1, and basket 2 to Zone 2 of the Ninja Foodi 2-Basket Air Fryer.
5. Choose the "Air Fry" mode for Zone 1 and set the temperature to 350 degrees F and 10 minutes of cooking time.
6. Select the "MATCH COOK" option to copy the settings for Zone 2.
7. Initiate cooking by pressing the START/PAUSE BUTTON.
8. Flip the squash once cooked halfway through.
9. Serve.

Nutrition:
- (Per serving) Calories 206 | Fat 3.4g |Sodium 174mg | Carbs 35g | Fiber 9.4g | Sugar 5.9g | Protein 10.6g

Bacon Potato Patties

Servings: 2
Cooking Time: 15 Minutes
Ingredients:
- 1 egg
- 600g mashed potatoes
- 119g breadcrumbs
- 2 bacon slices, cooked & chopped
- 235g cheddar cheese, shredded
- 15g flour
- Pepper
- Salt

Directions:
1. In a bowl, mix mashed potatoes with remaining ingredients until well combined.
2. Make patties from potato mixture and place on a plate.
3. Place plate in the refrigerator for 10 minutes
4. Insert a crisper plate in the Ninja Foodi air fryer baskets.
5. Place the prepared patties in both baskets.
6. Select zone 1 then select "air fry" mode and set the temperature to 390 degrees F for 15 minutes. Press "match" to match zone 2 settings to zone 1. Press "start/stop" to begin. Turn halfway through.

Nutrition:
- (Per serving) Calories 702 | Fat 26.8g |Sodium 1405mg | Carbs 84.8g | Fiber 2.7g | Sugar 3.8g | Protein 30.5g

Buffalo Bites

Servings: 6
Cooking Time: 30 Minutes
Ingredients:
- For the bites:
- 1 small cauliflower head, cut into florets
- 2 tablespoons olive oil
- 3 tablespoons buffalo wing sauce
- 3 tablespoons butter, melted
- For the dip:
- 1½ cups 2% cottage cheese
- ¼ cup fat-free plain Greek yogurt
- ¼ cup crumbled blue cheese
- 1 sachet ranch salad dressing mix
- Celery sticks (optional)

Directions:
1. In a large bowl, combine the cauliflower and oil; toss to coat.
2. Place a crisper plate in each drawer. Put the coated cauliflower florets in each drawer in a single layer. Place the drawers in the unit.
3. Select zone 1, then AIR FRY, then set the temperature to 360 degrees F/ 180 degrees C with a 15-minute timer. To match zone 2 settings to zone 1, choose MATCH. To begin, select START/STOP.
4. Remove the cauliflower from the drawers after the timer has finished.
5. Combine the buffalo sauce and melted butter in a large mixing bowl. Put in the cauliflower and toss to coat. Place on a serving dish and serve.
6. Combine the dip ingredients in a small bowl. Serve with the cauliflower and celery sticks, if desired.

Nutrition:
- (Per serving) Calories 203 | Fat 13g | Sodium 1470mg | Carbs 13g | Fiber 4g | Sugar 1g | Protein 9g

Air Fried Okra

Servings: 2
Cooking Time: 13 Minutes.
Ingredients:
- ½ lb. okra pods sliced
- 1 teaspoon olive oil
- ¼ teaspoon salt
- ⅛ teaspoon black pepper

Directions:
1. Preheat the Ninja Foodi Dual Zone Air Fryer to 350 degrees F.
2. Toss okra with olive oil, salt, and black pepper in a bowl.
3. Spread the okra in a single layer in the two crisper plates.
4. Return the crisper plate to the Ninja Foodi Dual Zone Air Fryer.
5. Choose the Air Fry mode for Zone 1 and set the temperature to 375 degrees F and the time to 13 minutes.
6. Select the "MATCH" button to copy the settings for Zone 2.
7. Initiate cooking by pressing the START/STOP button.
8. Toss the okra once cooked halfway through, and resume cooking.
9. Serve warm.

Nutrition:
- (Per serving) Calories 208 | Fat 5g | Sodium 1205mg | Carbs 34.1g | Fiber 7.8g | Sugar 2.5g | Protein 5.9g

Caprese Panini With Zucchini Chips

Servings: 4
Cooking Time: 20 Minutes
Ingredients:
- FOR THE PANINI
- 4 tablespoons pesto
- 8 slices Italian-style sandwich bread
- 1 tomato, diced
- 6 ounces fresh mozzarella cheese, shredded
- ¼ cup mayonnaise
- FOR THE ZUCCHINI CHIPS
- ½ cup all-purpose flour

The Complete Ninja Foodi Dual Zone Air Fryer Cookbook

- 2 large eggs
- ¼ teaspoon freshly ground black pepper
- ⅛ teaspoon kosher salt
- ½ cup panko bread crumbs
- ¼ cup grated Parmesan cheese
- 1 teaspoon Italian seasoning
- 1 medium zucchini, cut into ¼-inch-thick rounds
- 2 tablespoons vegetable oil

Directions:
1. To prep the panini: Spread 1 tablespoon of pesto each on 4 slices of the bread. Layer the diced tomato and shredded mozzarella on the other 4 slices of bread. Top the tomato/cheese mixture with the pesto-coated bread, pesto-side down, to form 4 sandwiches.
2. Spread the outside of each sandwich (both bread slices) with a thin layer of the mayonnaise.
3. To prep the zucchini chips: Set up a breading station with three small shallow bowls. Place the flour in the first bowl. In the second bowl, beat together the eggs, salt, and black pepper. Place the panko, Parmesan, and Italian seasoning in the third bowl.
4. Bread the zucchini in this order: First, dip the slices into the flour, coating both sides. Then, dip into the beaten egg. Finally, coat in the panko mixture. Drizzle the zucchini on both sides with the oil.
5. To cook the panini and zucchini chips: Install a crisper plate in each of the two baskets. Place 2 sandwiches in the Zone 1 basket and insert the basket in the unit. Place half of the zucchini chips in a single layer in the Zone 2 basket and insert the basket in the unit.
6. Select Zone 1, select AIR FRY, set the temperature to 375°F, and set the timer to 20 minutes.
7. Select Zone 2, select AIR FRY, set the temperature to 400°F, and set the timer to 20 minutes. Select SMART FINISH.
8. Press START/PAUSE to begin cooking.
9. When the Zone 1 timer reads 15 minutes, press START/PAUSE. Remove the basket, and use silicone-tipped tongs or a spatula to flip the sandwiches. Reinsert the basket and press START/PAUSE to resume cooking.
10. When both timers read 10 minutes, press START/PAUSE. Remove the Zone 1 basket and transfer the sandwiches to a plate. Place the remaining 2 sandwiches into the basket and insert the basket in the unit. Remove the Zone 2 basket and transfer the zucchini chips to a serving plate. Place the remaining zucchini chips in the basket. Reinsert the basket and press START/PAUSE to resume cooking.
11. When the Zone 1 timer reads 5 minutes, press START/PAUSE. Remove the basket and flip the sandwiches. Reinsert the basket and press START/PAUSE to resume cooking.
12. When cooking is complete, the panini should be toasted and the zucchini chips golden brown and crisp.
13. Cut each panini in half. Serve hot with zucchini chips on the side.

Nutrition:
- (Per serving) Calories: 751; Total fat: 39g; Saturated fat: 9.5g; Carbohydrates: 77g; Fiber: 3.5g; Protein: 23g; Sodium: 1,086mg

Bbq Corn

Servings: 4
Cooking Time: 10 Minutes
Ingredients:
- 450g can baby corn, drained & rinsed
- 56g BBQ sauce
- ½ tsp Sriracha sauce

Directions:
1. In a bowl, toss the baby corn with sriracha sauce and BBQ sauce until well coated.
2. Insert a crisper plate in the Ninja Foodi air fryer baskets.
3. Add the baby corn to both baskets.
4. Select zone 1, then select "air fry" mode and set the temperature to 390 degrees F for 10 minutes. Press "match" to match zone 2 settings to zone 1. Press "start/stop" to begin. Stir halfway through.

Nutrition:
- (Per serving) Calories 46 | Fat 0.1g | Sodium 446mg | Carbs 10.2g | Fiber 2.8g | Sugar 5.9g | Protein 0.9g

Fried Patty Pan Squash

Servings: 6
Cooking Time: 15 Minutes
Ingredients:
- 5 cups small pattypan squash, halved
- 1 tablespoon olive oil
- 2 garlic cloves, minced
- ½ teaspoon salt
- ¼ teaspoon dried oregano
- ¼ teaspoon dried thyme
- ¼ teaspoon pepper
- 1 tablespoon minced parsley

Directions:
1. Rub the squash with oil, garlic and the rest of the ingredients.
2. Spread the squash in the air fryer baskets.
3. Return the air fryer basket 1 to Zone 1, and basket 2 to Zone 2 of the Ninja Foodi 2-Basket Air Fryer.
4. Choose the "Air Fry" mode for Zone 1 at 375 degrees F and 15 minutes of cooking time.
5. Select the "MATCH COOK" option to copy the settings for Zone 2.
6. Initiate cooking by pressing the START/PAUSE BUTTON.
7. Flip the squash once cooked halfway through.
8. Garnish with parsley.
9. Serve warm.

Nutrition:
- (Per serving) Calories 208 | Fat 5g | Sodium 1205mg | Carbs 34.1g | Fiber 7.8g | Sugar 2.5g | Protein 5.9g

Stuffed Tomatoes

Servings: 2
Cooking Time: 8
Ingredients:
- 2 cups brown rice, cooked
- 1 cup of tofu, grilled and chopped
- 4 large red tomatoes
- 4 tablespoons basil, chopped
- 1/4 tablespoon olive oil
- Salt and black pepper, to taste
- 2 tablespoons of lemon juice
- 1 teaspoon of red chili powder
- ½ cup Parmesan cheese

Directions:
1. Take a large bowl and mix rice, tofu, basil, olive oil, salt, black pepper, lemon juice, and chili powder.
2. Take four large tomatoes and center core them.
3. Fill the cavity with the rice mixture.
4. Top it off with the cheese sprinkle.
5. Divide the tomatoes into two air fryer baskets.
6. turn on zone one basket and cook tomatoes at AIRFRY mode, for 8 minutes at 400 degrees F.
7. Select the MATCH button for zone two baskets, which cooks food by copying the setting across both zones.
8. Serve and enjoy.

Nutrition:
- (Per serving) Calories 1034| Fat 24.2g| Sodium 527mg | Carbs165 g | Fiber12.1 g | Sugar 1.2g | Protein 43.9g

Fried Avocado Tacos

Servings: 4
Cooking Time: 10 Minutes
Ingredients:
- For the sauce:
- 2 cups shredded fresh kale or coleslaw mix
- ¼ cup minced fresh cilantro
- ¼ cup plain Greek yogurt

The Complete Ninja Foodi Dual Zone Air Fryer Cookbook

- 2 tablespoons lime juice
- 1 teaspoon honey
- ¼ teaspoon salt
- ¼ teaspoon ground chipotle pepper
- ¼ teaspoon pepper
- For the tacos:
- 1 large egg, beaten
- ¼ cup cornmeal
- ½ teaspoon salt
- ½ teaspoon garlic powder
- ½ teaspoon ground chipotle pepper
- 2 medium avocados, peeled and sliced
- Cooking spray
- 8 flour tortillas or corn tortillas (6 inches), heated up
- 1 medium tomato, chopped
- Crumbled queso fresco (optional)

Directions:
1. Combine the first 8 ingredients in a bowl. Cover and refrigerate until serving.
2. Place the egg in a shallow bowl. In another shallow bowl, mix the cornmeal, salt, garlic powder, and chipotle pepper.
3. Dip the avocado slices in the egg, then into the cornmeal mixture, gently patting to help adhere.
4. Place a crisper plate in both drawers. Put the avocado slices in the drawers in a single layer. Insert the drawers into the unit.
5. Select zone 1, then AIR FRY, then set the temperature to 360 degrees F/ 180 degrees C with a 6-minute timer. To match zone 2 settings to zone 1, choose MATCH. To begin, select START/STOP.
6. Put the avocado slices, prepared sauce, tomato, and queso fresco in the tortillas and serve.

Nutrition:
- (Per serving) Calories 407 | Fat 21g | Sodium 738mg | Carbs 48g | Fiber 4g | Sugar 9g | Protein 9g

Green Salad With Crispy Fried Goat Cheese And Baked Croutons

Servings: 4
Cooking Time: 10 Minutes

Ingredients:
- FOR THE GOAT CHEESE
- 1 (4-ounce) log soft goat cheese
- ½ cup panko bread crumbs
- 2 tablespoons vegetable oil
- FOR THE CROUTONS
- 2 slices Italian-style sandwich bread
- 2 tablespoons vegetable oil
- 1 tablespoon poultry seasoning
- ½ teaspoon kosher salt
- ¼ teaspoon freshly ground black pepper
- FOR THE SALAD
- 8 cups green leaf lettuce leaves
- ½ cup store-bought balsamic vinaigrette

Directions:
1. To prep the goat cheese: Cut the goat cheese into 8 round slices.
2. Spread the panko on a plate. Gently press the cheese into the panko to coat on both sides. Drizzle with the oil.
3. To prep the croutons: Cut the bread into cubes and place them in a large bowl. Add the oil, poultry seasoning, salt, and black pepper. Mix well to coat the bread cubes evenly.
4. To cook the goat cheese and croutons: Install a crisper plate in each of the two baskets. Place the goat cheese in the Zone 1 basket and insert the basket in the unit. Place the croutons in the Zone 2 basket and insert the basket in the unit.
5. Select Zone 1, select AIR FRY, set the temperature to 400°F, and set the timer to 6 minutes.
6. Select Zone 2, select BAKE, set the temperature to 390°F, and set the timer to 10 minutes. Select SMART FINISH.
7. Press START/PAUSE to begin cooking.
8. When cooking is complete, the goat cheese will be golden brown and the croutons crisp.
9. Remove the Zone 1 basket. Let the goat cheese cool in the basket for 5 minutes; it will firm up as it cools.
10. To assemble the salad: In a large bowl, combine the lettuce, vinaigrette, and croutons. Toss well. Divide the salad among four plates. Top each plate with 2 pieces of goat cheese.

Nutrition:
- (Per serving) Calories: 578; Total fat: 40g; Saturated fat: 14g; Carbohydrates: 39g; Fiber: 3.5g; Protein: 24g; Sodium: 815mg

Satay-style Tempeh With Corn Fritters

Servings: 4
Cooking Time: 15 Minutes

Ingredients:

- FOR THE TEMPEH
- 1 (8-ounce) package tempeh
- 3 tablespoons fresh lemon juice, divided
- 2 tablespoons soy sauce, divided
- 2 garlic cloves, chopped
- ½ teaspoon ground turmeric
- 2 tablespoons vegetable oil
- ¾ cup canned full-fat coconut milk
- 4 tablespoons peanut butter
- 1 teaspoon light brown sugar
- ½ teaspoon red pepper flakes
- 1 scallion, chopped
- FOR THE CORN FRITTERS
- 2 cups frozen corn, thawed and drained
- 2 scallions, thinly sliced
- ¼ cup chopped fresh cilantro
- ¼ teaspoon kosher salt
- 2 large eggs
- ½ cup all-purpose flour
- 2 tablespoons vegetable oil

Directions:

1. To prep the tempeh: Slice the tempeh into ¼-inch-thick slabs.
2. In a large bowl, combine 2 tablespoons of lemon juice, 1 tablespoon of soy sauce, the garlic, turmeric, and oil.
3. Add the tempeh to the marinade and toss to coat the pieces. Let marinate for 15 minutes.
4. In a medium bowl, whisk together the coconut milk, peanut butter, remaining 1 tablespoon of lemon juice, remaining 1 tablespoon of soy sauce, brown sugar, red pepper flakes, and scallion. Set aside.
5. To prep the corn fritters: In a large bowl, combine the corn, scallions, cilantro, and salt. Mix in the eggs and flour until everything is well combined.
6. To cook the tempeh and fritters: Install a broil rack in the Zone 1 basket. Arrange the tempeh in a single layer on the rack and insert the basket in the unit. Install a crisper plate in the Zone 2 basket. Spoon 2 tablespoons of corn fritter batter into each corner of the basket and drizzle with oil. Flatten slightly with the back of the spoon and insert the basket in the unit.
7. Select Zone 1, select AIR BROIL, set the temperature to 400°F, and set the timer to 8 minutes.
8. Select Zone 2, select AIR FRY, set the temperature to 375°F, and set the timer to 15 minutes. Select SMART FINISH.
9. Press START/PAUSE to begin cooking.
10. When the Zone 2 timer reads 5 minutes, press START/PAUSE. Remove the basket and use silicone-tipped tongs or a spatula to flip the corn fritters. Reinsert the basket and press START/PAUSE to resume cooking.
11. When cooking is complete, the tempeh will be golden brown and the corn fritters set in the center and browned on the edges.
12. Serve the tempeh with the peanut sauce for dipping and the corn fritters on the side.

Nutrition:

- (Per serving) Calories: 578; Total fat: 40g; Saturated fat: 14g; Carbohydrates: 39g; Fiber: 3.5g; Protein: 24g; Sodium: 815mg

Broccoli, Squash, & Pepper

Servings: 4
Cooking Time: 12 Minutes
Ingredients:
- 175g broccoli florets
- 1 red bell pepper, diced
- 1 tbsp olive oil
- ½ tsp garlic powder
- ¼ onion, sliced
- 1 zucchini, sliced
- 2 yellow squash, sliced
- Pepper
- Salt

Directions:
1. In a bowl, toss veggies with oil, garlic powder, pepper, and salt.
2. Insert a crisper plate in the Ninja Foodi air fryer baskets.
3. Add the vegetable mixture in both baskets.
4. Select zone 1 then select "air fry" mode and set the temperature to 390 degrees F for 12 minutes. Press "match" to match zone 2 settings to zone 1. Press "start/stop" to begin. Stir halfway through.

Nutrition:
- (Per serving) Calories 75 | Fat 3.9g |Sodium 62mg | Carbs 9.6g | Fiber 2.8g | Sugar 4.8g | Protein 2.9g

Quinoa Patties

Servings: 4
Cooking Time: 32 Minutes.
Ingredients:
- 1 cup quinoa red
- 1½ cups water
- 1 teaspoon salt
- black pepper, ground
- 1½ cups rolled oats
- 3 eggs beaten
- ¼ cup minced white onion
- ½ cup crumbled feta cheese
- ¼ cup chopped fresh chives
- Salt and black pepper, to taste
- Vegetable or canola oil
- 4 hamburger buns
- 4 arugulas
- 4 slices tomato sliced
- Cucumber yogurt dill sauce
- 1 cup cucumber, diced
- 1 cup Greek yogurt
- 2 teaspoons lemon juice
- ¼ teaspoon salt
- Black pepper, ground
- 1 tablespoon chopped fresh dill
- 1 tablespoon olive oil

Directions:
1. Add quinoa to a saucepan filled with cold water, salt, and black pepper, and place it over medium-high heat.
2. Cook the quinoa to a boil, then reduce the heat, cover, and cook for 20 minutes on a simmer.
3. Fluff and mix the cooked quinoa with a fork and remove it from the heat.
4. Spread the quinoa in a baking stay.
5. Mix eggs, oats, onion, herbs, cheese, salt, and black pepper.
6. Stir in quinoa, then mix well. Make 4 patties out of this quinoa cheese mixture.
7. Divide the patties in the two crisper plates and spray them with cooking oil.
8. Return the crisper plates to the Ninja Foodi Dual Zone Air Fryer.
9. Choose the Air Fry mode for Zone 1 and set the temperature to 390 degrees F and the time to 13 minutes.
10. Select the "MATCH" button to copy the settings for Zone 2.
11. Initiate cooking by pressing the START/STOP button.
12. Flip the patties once cooked halfway through, and resume cooking.
13. Meanwhile, prepare the cucumber yogurt dill sauce by mixing all of its ingredients in a mixing bowl.
14. Place each quinoa patty in a burger bun along with arugula leaves.
15. Serve with yogurt dill sauce.

Nutrition:
- (Per serving) Calories 231 | Fat 9g |Sodium 271mg | Carbs 32.8g | Fiber 6.4g | Sugar 7g | Protein 6.3g

Buffalo Seitan With Crispy Zucchini Noodles

Servings: 4
Cooking Time: 12 Minutes

Ingredients:
- FOR THE BUFFALO SEITAN
- 1 (8-ounce) package precooked seitan strips
- 1 teaspoon garlic powder, divided
- ½ teaspoon onion powder
- ¼ teaspoon smoked paprika
- ¼ cup Louisiana-style hot sauce
- 2 tablespoons vegetable oil
- 1 tablespoon tomato paste
- ¼ teaspoon freshly ground black pepper
- FOR THE ZUCCHINI NOODLES
- 3 large egg whites
- 1¼ cups all-purpose flour
- 1 teaspoon kosher salt, divided
- 12 ounces seltzer water or club soda
- 5 ounces zucchini noodles
- Nonstick cooking spray

Directions:
1. To prep the Buffalo seitan: Season the seitan strips with ½ teaspoon of garlic powder, the onion powder, and smoked paprika.
2. In a large bowl, whisk together the hot sauce, oil, tomato paste, remaining ½ teaspoon of garlic powder, and the black pepper. Set the bowl of Buffalo sauce aside.
3. To prep the zucchini noodles: In a medium bowl, use a handheld mixer to beat the egg whites until stiff peaks form.
4. In a large bowl, combine the flour and ½ teaspoon of salt. Mix in the seltzer to form a thin batter. Fold in the beaten egg whites.
5. Add the zucchini to the batter and gently mix to coat.
6. To cook the seitan and zucchini noodles: Install a crisper plate in each of the two baskets. Place the seitan in the Zone 1 basket and insert the basket in the unit. Lift the noodles from the batter one at a time, letting the excess drip off, and place them in the Zone 2 basket. Insert the basket in the unit.
7. Select Zone 1, select BAKE, set the temperature to 370°F, and set the timer to 12 minutes.
8. Select Zone 2, select AIR FRY, set the temperature to 400°F, and set the timer to 12 minutes. Select SMART FINISH.
9. Press START/PAUSE to begin cooking.
10. When the Zone 1 timer reads 2 minutes, press START/PAUSE. Remove the basket and transfer the seitan to the bowl of Buffalo sauce. Turn to coat, then return the seitan to the basket. Reinsert the basket and press START/PAUSE to resume cooking.
11. When cooking is complete, the seitan should be warmed through and the zucchini noodles crisp and light golden brown.
12. Sprinkle the zucchini noodles with the remaining ½ teaspoon of salt. If desired, drizzle extra Buffalo sauce over the seitan. Serve hot.

Nutrition:
- (Per serving) Calories: 252; Total fat: 15g; Saturated fat: 1g; Carbohydrates: 22g; Fiber: 1.5g; Protein: 13g; Sodium: 740mg

Chapter 6: Beef, Pork, And Lamb Recipes

Nigerian Peanut-crusted Bavette Steak

Servings: 4
Cooking Time: 8 Minutes

Ingredients:

- Suya Spice Mix:
- 60 ml dry-roasted peanuts
- 1 teaspoon cumin seeds
- 1 teaspoon garlic powder
- 1 teaspoon smoked paprika
- ½ teaspoon ground ginger
- 1 teaspoon coarse or flaky salt
- ½ teaspoon cayenne pepper
- Steak:
- 450 g bavette or skirt steak
- 2 tablespoons vegetable oil

Directions:

1. For the spice mix: In a clean coffee grinder or spice mill, combine the peanuts and cumin seeds. Process until you get a coarse powder. 2. Pour the peanut mixture into a small bowl, add the garlic powder, paprika, ginger, salt, and cayenne, and stir to combine. This recipe makes about 120 ml suya spice mix. Store leftovers in an airtight container in a cool, dry place for up to 1 month. 3. For the steak: Cut the steak into ½-inch-thick slices, cutting against the grain and at a slight angle. Place the beef strips in a resealable plastic bag and add the oil and 2½ to 3 tablespoons of the spice mixture. Seal the bag and massage to coat all of the meat with the oil and spice mixture. Marinate at room temperature for 30 minutes or in the refrigerator for up to 24 hours. 4. Place the beef strips in the zone 1 air fryer drawer. Set the temperature to 204°C for 8 minutes, turning the strips halfway through the cooking time. 5. Transfer the meat to a serving platter. Sprinkle with additional spice mix, if desired.

Mongolian Beef With Sweet Chili Brussels Sprouts

Servings: 4
Cooking Time: 20 Minutes

Ingredients:

- FOR THE MONGOLIAN BEEF
- 1 pound flank steak, cut into thin strips
- 1 tablespoon olive oil
- 2 tablespoons cornstarch
- ½ cup reduced-sodium soy sauce
- ½ cup packed light brown sugar
- 1 tablespoon chili paste (optional)
- 1 tablespoon minced garlic
- 1 tablespoon minced fresh ginger
- 2 scallions, chopped
- FOR THE BRUSSELS SPROUTS
- 1 pound Brussels sprouts, halved lengthwise
- 1 tablespoon olive oil
- ½ cup gochujang sauce
- 2 tablespoons rice vinegar
- 1 tablespoon reduced-sodium soy sauce
- 1 tablespoon light brown sugar
- 1 teaspoon fresh garlic

Directions:

1. To prep the Mongolian beef: In a large bowl, combine the flank steak and olive oil and toss to coat. Add the cornstarch and toss to coat.
2. In a small bowl, whisk together the soy sauce, brown sugar, chili paste (if using), garlic, and ginger. Set the soy sauce mixture aside.
3. To prep the Brussels sprouts: In a large bowl, combine the Brussels sprouts and oil and toss to coat.
4. In a small bowl, whisk together the gochujang sauce, vinegar, soy sauce, brown sugar, and garlic. Set the chili sauce mixture aside.
5. To cook the beef and Brussels sprouts: Install a crisper plate in each of the two baskets. Place the beef in the Zone 1 basket and insert the basket in the unit. Place the Brussels sprouts in the Zone 2 basket and insert the basket in the unit.
6. Select Zone 1, select AIR FRY, set the temperature to 390°F, and set the time to 15 minutes.
7. Select Zone 2, select AIR FRY, set the temperature to 400°F, and set the time to 20 minutes. Select SMART FINISH.
8. Press START/PAUSE to begin cooking.

9. When both timers read 5 minutes, press START/PAUSE. Remove the Zone 1 basket, add the reserved soy sauce mixture and the scallions, and toss with the beef. Reinsert the basket. Remove the Zone 2 basket, add the reserved chili sauce mixture, and toss with the Brussels sprouts. Reinsert the basket and press START/PAUSE to resume cooking.
10. When cooking is complete, the steak should be cooked through and the Brussels sprouts tender and slightly caramelized. Serve warm.

Nutrition:
- (Per serving) Calories: 481; Total fat: 16g; Saturated fat: 4.5g; Carbohydrates: 60g; Fiber: 5g; Protein: 27g; Sodium: 2,044mg

Stuffed Beef Fillet With Feta Cheese

Servings: 4
Cooking Time: 10 Minutes

Ingredients:
- 680 g beef fillet, pounded to ¼ inch thick
- 3 teaspoons sea salt
- 1 teaspoon ground black pepper
- 60 g creamy goat cheese
- 120 ml crumbled feta cheese
- 60 ml finely chopped onions
- 2 cloves garlic, minced
- Cooking spray

Directions:
1. Preheat the air fryer to 204°C. Spritz the two air fryer drawers with cooking spray. 2. Unfold the beef on a clean work surface. Rub the salt and pepper all over the beef to season. 3. Make the filling for the stuffed beef fillet: Combine the goat cheese, feta, onions, and garlic in a medium bowl. Stir until well blended. 4. Spoon the mixture in the center of the fillet. Roll the fillet up tightly like rolling a burrito and use some kitchen twine to tie the fillet. 5. Arrange the fillet in the two air fryer drawers and air fry for 10 minutes, flipping the fillet halfway through to ensure even cooking, or until an instant-read thermometer inserted in the center of the fillet registers 57°C for medium-rare. 6. Transfer to a platter and serve immediately.

Bacon-wrapped Cheese Pork

Servings: 4
Cooking Time: 20 Minutes

Ingredients:
- 4 (1-inch-thick) boneless pork chops
- 2 (150 g) packages Boursin cheese
- 8 slices thin-cut bacon

Directions:
1. Spray the air fryer drawer with avocado oil. Preheat the air fryer to 204°C.
2. Place one of the chops on a cutting board. With a sharp knife held parallel to the cutting board, make a 1-inch-wide incision on the top edge of the chop. Carefully cut into the chop to form a large pocket, leaving a ½-inch border along the sides and bottom. Repeat with the other 3 chops.
3. Snip the corner of a large resealable plastic bag to form a ¾-inch hole. Place the Boursin cheese in the bag and pipe the cheese into the pockets in the chops, dividing the cheese evenly among them.
4. Wrap 2 slices of bacon around each chop and secure the ends with toothpicks. Place the bacon-wrapped chops in the two air fryer drawers and cook for 10 minutes, then flip the chops and cook for another 8 to 10 minutes, until the bacon is crisp, the chops are cooked through, and the internal temperature reaches 64°C.
5. Store leftovers in an airtight container in the refrigerator for up to 3 days. Reheat in a preheated 204°C air fryer for 5 minutes, or until warmed through.

Glazed Steak Recipe

Servings: 2
Cooking Time: 25

Ingredients:
- 1 pound of beef steaks
- ½ cup, soy sauce
- Salt and black pepper, to taste
- 1 tablespoon of vegetable oil

- 1 teaspoon of grated ginger
- 4 cloves garlic, minced
- 1/4 cup brown sugar

Directions:
1. Take a bowl and whisk together soy sauce, salt, pepper, vegetable oil, garlic, brown sugar, and ginger.
2. Once a paste is made rub the steak with the marinate
3. Let it sit for 30 minutes.
4. After 30 minutes add the steak to the air fryer basket and set it to AIR BROIL mode at 400 degrees F for 18-22 minutes.
5. After 10 minutes, hit pause and takeout the basket.
6. Let the steak flip and again let it AIR BROIL for the remaining minutes.
7. Once 25 minutes of cooking cycle completes.
8. Take out the steak and let it rest. Serve by cutting into slices.
9. Enjoy.

Nutrition:
- (Per serving) Calories 563| Fat 21 g| Sodium 156mg | Carbs 20.6g | Fiber0.3 g| Sugar17.8 g | Protein69.4 g

Sausage And Cauliflower Arancini

Servings: 6
Cooking Time: 28 To 32 Minutes
Ingredients:
- Avocado oil spray
- 170 g Italian-seasoned sausage, casings removed
- 60 ml diced onion
- 1 teaspoon minced garlic
- 1 teaspoon dried thyme
- Sea salt and freshly ground black pepper, to taste
- 120 ml cauliflower rice
- 85 g cream cheese
- 110 g Cheddar cheese, shredded
- 1 large egg
- 120 ml finely ground blanched almond flour
- 60 ml finely grated Parmesan cheese
- Keto-friendly marinara sauce, for serving

Directions:
1. Spray a large skillet with oil and place it over medium-high heat. Once the skillet is hot, put the sausage in the skillet and cook for 7 minutes, breaking up the meat with the back of a spoon.
2. Reduce the heat to medium and add the onion. Cook for 5 minutes, then add the garlic, thyme, and salt and pepper to taste. Cook for 1 minute more.
3. Add the cauliflower rice and cream cheese to the skillet. Cook for 7 minutes, stirring frequently, until the cream cheese melts and the cauliflower is tender.
4. Remove the skillet from the heat and stir in the Cheddar cheese. Using a cookie scoop, form the mixture into 1½-inch balls. Place the balls on a parchment paper-lined baking sheet. Freeze for 30 minutes.
5. Place the egg in a shallow bowl and beat it with a fork. In a separate bowl, stir together the almond flour and Parmesan cheese.
6. Dip the cauliflower balls into the egg, then coat them with the almond flour mixture, gently pressing the mixture to the balls to adhere.
7. Set the air fryer to 204ºC. Spray the cauliflower rice balls with oil, and arrange them in a single layer in the two air fryer drawers. Air fry for 5 minutes. Flip the rice balls and spray them with more oil. Air fry for 3 to 7 minutes longer, until the balls are golden brown.
8. Serve warm with marinara sauce.

Goat Cheese-stuffed Bavette Steak

Servings: 6
Cooking Time: 14 Minutes
Ingredients:
- 450 g bavette or skirt steak
- 1 tablespoon avocado oil
- ½ teaspoon sea salt
- ½ teaspoon garlic powder

- ¼ teaspoon freshly ground black pepper
- 60 g goat cheese, crumbled
- 235 ml baby spinach, chopped

Directions:
1. Place the steak in a large zip-top bag or between two pieces of plastic wrap. Using a meat mallet or heavy-bottomed skillet, pound the steak to an even ¼-inch thickness.
2. Brush both sides of the steak with the avocado oil.
3. Mix the salt, garlic powder, and pepper in a small dish. Sprinkle this mixture over both sides of the steak.
4. Sprinkle the goat cheese over top, and top that with the spinach.
5. Starting at one of the long sides, roll the steak up tightly. Tie the rolled steak with kitchen string at 3-inch intervals.
6. Set the zone 1 air fryer drawer to 204ºC. Place the steak roll-up in the zone 1 air fryer drawer. Air fry for 7 minutes. Flip the steak and cook for an additional 7 minutes, until an instant-read thermometer reads 49ºC for medium-rare .

Pigs In A Blanket With Spinach-artichoke Stuffed Mushrooms

Servings:4
Cooking Time: 15 Minutes

Ingredients:
- FOR THE PIGS IN A BLANKET
- Half an 8-ounce tube refrigerated crescent roll dough
- 4 hot dogs
- ½ teaspoon everything bagel seasoning (optional)
- FOR THE STUFFED MUSHROOMS
- 1 cup frozen chopped spinach, thawed and drained
- 1 (14-ounce) can artichoke hearts, drained and chopped
- 2 ounces (¼ cup) cream cheese, at room temperature
- ¼ cup grated Parmesan cheese
- ½ teaspoon garlic powder
- 1 (8-ounce) package whole cremini mushrooms, stems removed

Directions:
1. To prep the pigs in a blanket: Unroll the crescent roll dough. It will be scored into 4 triangular pieces, but leave them in place and pinch together at the seams to form 1 large square of dough. Cut the dough into 4 strips.
2. Wrap one strip of dough around each hot dog, starting with a short end of the strips and wrapping in a spiral motion around the hot dog. If desired, sprinkle each pig in a blanket with everything bagel seasoning.
3. To prep the stuffed mushrooms: In a medium bowl, combine the spinach, artichoke hearts, cream cheese, Parmesan, and garlic powder. Stuff about 1 tablespoon of filling into each mushroom cap.
4. To cook the pigs in a blanket and mushrooms: Install a crisper plate in each of the two baskets. Place the pigs in a blanket in the Zone 1 basket and insert the basket in the unit. Place the mushrooms in the Zone 2 basket and insert the basket in the unit.
5. Select Zone 1, select AIR FRY, set the temperature to 370°F, and set the time to 8 minutes.
6. Select Zone 2, select BAKE, set the temperature to 370°F, and set the time to 15 minutes. Select SMART FINISH.
7. Press START/PAUSE to begin cooking.
8. When cooking is complete, the crescent roll dough should be cooked through and golden brown, and the mushrooms should be tender.

Nutrition:
- (Per serving) Calories: 371; Total fat: 25g; Saturated fat: 11g; Carbohydrates: 22g; Fiber: 2.5g; Protein: 14g; Sodium: 1,059mg

Beef And Bean Taquitos With Mexican Rice

Servings:4
Cooking Time: 15 Minutes

Ingredients:
- FOR THE TAQUITOS
- ½ pound ground beef (85 percent lean)
- 1 tablespoon taco seasoning
- 8 (6-inch) soft white corn tortillas
- Nonstick cooking spray
- ¾ cup canned refried beans
- ½ cup shredded Mexican blend cheese (optional)
- FOR THE MEXICAN RICE
- 1 cup dried instant white rice (not microwavable)
- 1½ cups chicken broth

- ¼ cup jarred salsa
- 2 tablespoons canned tomato sauce
- 1 tablespoon vegetable oil
- ½ teaspoon kosher salt

Directions:
1. To prep the taquitos: In a large bowl, mix the ground beef and taco seasoning until well combined.
2. Mist both sides of each tortilla lightly with cooking spray.
3. To prep the Mexican rice: In the Zone 2 basket, combine the rice, broth, salsa, tomato sauce, oil, and salt. Stir well to ensure all of the rice is submerged in the liquid.
4. To cook the taquitos and rice: Install a crisper plate in the Zone 1 basket. Place the seasoned beef in the basket and insert the basket in the unit. Insert the Zone 2 basket in the unit.
5. Select Zone 1, select AIR FRY, set the temperature to 390°F, and set the time to 15 minutes.
6. Select Zone 2, select BAKE, set the temperature to 350°F, and set the time to 10 minutes. Select SMART FINISH.
7. Press START/PAUSE to begin cooking.
8. When the Zone 1 timer reads 10 minutes, press START/PAUSE. Remove the basket and transfer the beef to a medium bowl. Add the refried beans and cheese (if using) and combine well. Spoon 2 tablespoons of the filling onto each tortilla and roll tightly. Place the taquitos in the Zone 1 basket seam-side down. Reinsert the basket in the unit and press START/PAUSE to resume cooking.
9. When cooking is complete, the taquitos should be crisp and golden brown and the rice cooked through. Serve hot.

Nutrition:
- (Per serving) Calories: 431; Total fat: 18g; Saturated fat: 4g; Carbohydrates: 52g; Fiber: 5.5g; Protein: 18g; Sodium: 923mg

Kielbasa Sausage With Pineapple And Kheema Meatloaf

Servings: 6 To 8
Cooking Time: 15 Minutes

Ingredients:
- Kielbasa Sausage with Pineapple:
- 340 g kielbasa sausage, cut into ½-inch slices
- 1 (230 g) can pineapple chunks in juice, drained
- 235 ml pepper chunks
- 1 tablespoon barbecue seasoning
- 1 tablespoon soy sauce
- Cooking spray
- Kheema Meatloaf:
- 450 g 85% lean beef mince
- 2 large eggs, lightly beaten
- 235 ml diced brown onion
- 60 ml chopped fresh coriander
- 1 tablespoon minced fresh ginger
- 1 tablespoon minced garlic
- 2 teaspoons garam masala
- 1 teaspoon coarse or flaky salt
- 1 teaspoon ground turmeric
- 1 teaspoon cayenne pepper
- ½ teaspoon ground cinnamon
- ⅛ teaspoon ground cardamom

Directions:
1. Make the Kielbasa Sausage with Pineapple :
2. Preheat the air fryer to 200ºC. Spritz the zone 1 air fryer drawer with cooking spray.
3. Combine all the ingredients in a large bowl. Toss to mix well.
4. Pour the sausage mixture in the preheated zone 1 air fryer drawer.
5. Air fry for 10 minutes or until the sausage is lightly browned and the pepper and pineapple are soft. Shake the drawer halfway through. Serve immediately.
6. Make the Kheema Meatloaf :
7. In a large bowl, gently mix the beef mince, eggs, onion, coriander, ginger, garlic, garam masala, salt, turmeric, cayenne, cinnamon, and cardamom until thoroughly combined.
8. Place the seasoned meat in a baking pan. Place the pan in the zone 2 air fryer drawer. Set the temperature to 176ºC for 15 minutes. Use a meat thermometer to ensure the meat loaf has reached an internal temperature of 72ºC .
9. Drain the fat and liquid from the pan and let stand for 5 minutes before slicing.
10. Slice and serve hot.

Garlic-rosemary Pork Loin With Scalloped Potatoes And Cauliflower

Servings: 6
Cooking Time: 50 Minutes
Ingredients:
- FOR THE PORK LOIN
- 2 pounds pork loin roast
- 2 tablespoons vegetable oil
- 2 teaspoons dried thyme
- 2 teaspoons dried crushed rosemary
- 1 teaspoon minced garlic
- ¾ teaspoon kosher salt
- FOR THE SCALLOPED POTATOES AND CAULIFLOWER
- 1 teaspoon vegetable oil
- ¾ pound Yukon Gold potatoes, peeled and very thinly sliced
- 1½ cups cauliflower florets
- ¼ teaspoon kosher salt
- ¼ teaspoon freshly ground black pepper
- 1 tablespoon very cold unsalted butter, grated
- 3 tablespoons all-purpose flour
- 1 cup whole milk
- 1 cup shredded Gruyère cheese

Directions:
1. To prep the pork loin: Coat the pork with the oil. Season with thyme, rosemary, garlic, and salt.
2. To prep the potatoes and cauliflower: Brush the bottom and sides of the Zone 2 basket with the oil. Add one-third of the potatoes to the bottom of the basket and arrange in a single layer. Top with ½ cup of cauliflower florets. Sprinkle a third of the salt and black pepper on top. Scatter one-third of the butter on top and sprinkle on 1 tablespoon of flour. Repeat this step twice more for a total of three layers.
3. Pour the milk over the layered potatoes and cauliflower; it should just cover the top layer. Top with the Gruyère.
4. To cook the pork and scalloped vegetables: Install a crisper plate in the Zone 1 basket. Place the pork loin in the basket and insert the basket in the unit. Insert the Zone 2 basket in the unit.
5. Select Zone 1, select AIR FRY, set the temperature to 390°F, and set the time to 50 minutes.
6. Select Zone 2, select BAKE, set the temperature to 350°F, and set the time to 45 minutes. Select SMART FINISH.
7. Press START/PAUSE to begin cooking.
8. When cooking is complete, the pork will be cooked through (an instant-read thermometer should read 145°F) and the potatoes and cauliflower will be tender.
9. Let the pork rest for at least 15 minutes before slicing and serving with the scalloped vegetables.

Nutrition:
- (Per serving) Calories: 439; Total fat: 25g; Saturated fat: 10g; Carbohydrates: 17g; Fiber: 1.5g; Protein: 37g; Sodium: 431mg

Kheema Burgers

Servings: 4
Cooking Time: 12 Minutes
Ingredients:
- Burgers:
- 450 g 85% lean beef mince or lamb mince
- 2 large eggs, lightly beaten
- 1 medium brown onion, diced
- 60 ml chopped fresh coriander
- 1 tablespoon minced fresh ginger
- 3 cloves garlic, minced
- 2 teaspoons garam masala
- 1 teaspoon ground turmeric
- ½ teaspoon ground cinnamon
- ⅛ teaspoon ground cardamom
- 1 teaspoon coarse or flaky salt
- 1 teaspoon cayenne pepper
- Raita Sauce:
- 235 ml grated cucumber
- 120 ml sour cream
- ¼ teaspoon coarse or flaky salt
- ¼ teaspoon black pepper
- For Serving:
- 4 lettuce leaves, hamburger buns, or naan breads

Directions:
1. For the burgers: In a large bowl, combine the beef mince, eggs, onion, coriander, ginger, garlic, garam masala, turmeric, cinnamon, cardamom, salt, and cayenne. Gently mix until ingredients are thoroughly combined. 2. Divide the

meat into four portions and form into round patties. Make a slight depression in the middle of each patty with your thumb to prevent them from puffing up into a dome shape while cooking. 3. Place the patties in the zone 1 air fryer drawer. Set the temperature to 176°C for 12 minutes. Use a meat thermometer to ensure the burgers have reached an internal temperature of 72°C . 4. Meanwhile, for the sauce: In a small bowl, combine the cucumber, sour cream, salt, and pepper. 5. To serve: Place the burgers on the lettuce, buns, or naan and top with the sauce.

Meatballs

Servings: 4
Cooking Time: 20 Minutes
Ingredients:
- 450g ground beef
- 59ml milk
- 45g parmesan cheese, grated
- 50g breadcrumbs
- ½ tsp Italian seasoning
- 2 garlic cloves, minced
- Pepper
- Salt

Directions:
1. In a bowl, mix the meat and remaining ingredients until well combined.
2. Insert a crisper plate in the Ninja Foodi air fryer baskets.
3. Make small balls from the meat mixture and place them in both baskets.
4. Select zone 1, then select "air fry" mode and set the temperature to 375 degrees F for 15 minutes. Press "match" and "start/stop" to begin.

Nutrition:
- (Per serving) Calories 426 | Fat 17.3g |Sodium 820mg | Carbs 11.1g | Fiber 0.7g | Sugar 1.6g | Protein 48.8g

Easy Breaded Pork Chops

Servings: 8
Cooking Time: 12 Minutes
Ingredients:
- 1 egg
- 118ml milk
- 8 pork chops
- 1 packet ranch seasoning
- 238g breadcrumbs
- Pepper
- Salt

Directions:
1. In a small bowl, whisk the egg and milk.
2. In a separate shallow dish, mix breadcrumbs, ranch seasoning, pepper, and salt.
3. Dip each pork chop in the egg mixture, then coat with breadcrumbs.
4. Insert a crisper plate in the Ninja Foodi air fryer baskets.
5. Place the coated pork chops in both baskets.
6. Select zone 1, then select air fry mode and set the temperature to 360 degrees F for 12 minutes. Press "match" to match zone 2 settings to zone 1. Press "start/stop" to begin. Turn halfway through.

Nutrition:
- (Per serving) Calories 378 | Fat 22.2g |Sodium 298mg | Carbs 20.2g | Fiber 1.2g | Sugar 2.4g | Protein 22.8g

Simple Lamb Meatballs

Servings: 4
Cooking Time: 15 Minutes
Ingredients:
- 1-pound ground lamb
- 1 teaspoon ground cinnamon
- 1 teaspoon ground cumin
- 2 teaspoons granulated onion
- 2 tablespoons fresh parsley
- Salt and black pepper, to taste

Directions:
1. Add ground lamb, onion, cinnamon, cumin, parsley, salt and pepper in a large bowl. Mix until well combined.

2. Make 1-inch balls from the mixture and set aside.
3. Grease each basket of "Zone 1" and "Zone 2" of Ninja Foodi 2-Basket Air Fryer.
4. Press "Zone 1" and "Zone 2" and then rotate the knob for each zone to select "Air Fry".
5. Set the temperature to 380 degrees F/ 195 degrees C for both zones and then set the time for 5 minutes to preheat.
6. After preheating, arrange the meatballs into the basket of each zone.
7. Slide each basket into Air Fryer and set the time for 12 minutes.
8. Flip the meatballs once halfway through.
9. Take out and serve warm.

Breaded Pork Chops

Servings: 4
Cooking Time: 10 Minutes
Ingredients:
- 4 boneless, center-cut pork chops, 1-inch thick
- 1 teaspoon Cajun seasoning
- 1½ cups cheese and garlic-flavored croutons
- 2 eggs
- Cooking spray

Directions:
1. Season both sides of the pork chops with the Cajun seasoning on a platter.
2. In a small food processor, pulse the croutons until finely chopped; transfer to a shallow plate.
3. In a separate shallow bowl, lightly beat the eggs.
4. Dip the pork chops in the egg, allowing any excess to drip off. Then place the chops in the crouton crumbs. Coat the chops in cooking spray.
5. Install a crisper plate in both drawers. Place half the pork chops in the zone 1 drawer and half in zone 2's, then insert the drawers into the unit.
6. Select zone 1, select ROAST, set temperature to 390 degrees F/ 200 degrees C, and set time to 10 minutes. Select MATCH to match zone 2 settings to zone 1. Press the START/STOP button to begin cooking.
7. When the time reaches 6 minutes, press START/STOP to pause the unit. Remove the drawers and flip the chops. Reinsert the drawers into the unit and press START/STOP to resume cooking.
8. When cooking is complete, serve and enjoy!

Nutrition:
- (Per serving) Calories 394 | Fat 18.1g | Sodium 428mg | Carbs 10g | Fiber 0.8g | Sugar 0.9g | Protein 44.7g

Balsamic Steak Tips With Roasted Asparagus And Mushroom Medley

Servings: 4
Cooking Time: 25 Minutes
Ingredients:
- FOR THE STEAK TIPS
- 1½ pounds sirloin tips
- ½ cup olive oil
- ¼ cup balsamic vinegar
- ¼ cup packed light brown sugar
- 1 tablespoon reduced-sodium soy sauce
- 1 teaspoon finely chopped fresh rosemary
- 1 teaspoon minced garlic
- FOR THE ASPARAGUS AND MUSHROOMS
- 6 ounces sliced cremini mushrooms
- 1 small red onion, sliced
- 1 tablespoon olive oil
- 1 pound asparagus, tough ends trimmed
- ⅛ teaspoon kosher salt

Directions:
1. To prep the steak tips: In a large bowl, combine the sirloin tips, oil, vinegar, brown sugar, soy sauce, rosemary, and garlic. Mix well to coat the steak.
2. To prep the mushrooms: In a large bowl, combine the mushrooms, onion, and oil.
3. To cook the steak and vegetables: Install a crisper plate in each of the two baskets. Shake any excess marinade from the steak tips, place the steak in the Zone 1 basket, and insert the basket in the unit. Place the mushrooms and onions in the Zone 2 basket and insert the basket in the unit.
4. Select Zone 1, select AIR FRY, set the temperature to 400°F, and set the time to 12 minutes.

5. Select Zone 2, select ROAST, set the temperature to 400°F, and set the time to 25 minutes. Select SMART FINISH.
6. Press START/PAUSE to begin cooking.
7. When the Zone 2 timer reads 10 minutes, press START/PAUSE. Remove the basket, add the asparagus to the mushrooms and onion, and sprinkle with salt. Reinsert the basket and press START/PAUSE to resume cooking.
8. When cooking is complete, the beef should be cooked to your liking and the asparagus crisp-tender. Serve warm.

Nutrition:
- (Per serving) Calories: 524; Total fat: 33g; Saturated fat: 2.5g; Carbohydrates: 16g; Fiber: 3g; Protein: 41g; Sodium: 192mg

Minute Steak Roll-ups

Servings: 4
Cooking Time: 8 To 10 Minutes

Ingredients:
- 4 minute steaks (170 g each)
- 1 (450 g) bottle Italian dressing
- 1 teaspoon salt
- ½ teaspoon freshly ground black pepper
- 120 ml finely chopped brown onion
- 120 ml finely chopped green pepper
- 120 ml finely chopped mushrooms
- 1 to 2 tablespoons oil

Directions:
1. In a large resealable bag or airtight storage container, combine the steaks and Italian dressing. Seal the bag and refrigerate to marinate for 2 hours.
2. Remove the steaks from the marinade and place them on a cutting board. Discard the marinade. Evenly season the steaks with salt and pepper.
3. In a small bowl, stir together the onion, pepper, and mushrooms. Sprinkle the onion mixture evenly over the steaks. Roll up the steaks, jelly roll-style, and secure with toothpicks.
4. Preheat the air fryer to 204°C.
5. Place the steaks in the two air fryer drawers.
6. Cook for 4 minutes. Flip the steaks and spritz them with oil. Cook for 4 to 6 minutes more until the internal temperature reaches 64°C. Let rest for 5 minutes before serving.

Juicy Pork Chops

Servings: 4
Cooking Time: 15 Minutes

Ingredients:
- 450g pork chops
- ¼ tsp garlic powder
- 15ml olive oil
- ¼ tsp smoked paprika
- Pepper
- Salt

Directions:
1. In a small bowl, mix the garlic powder, paprika, pepper, and salt.
2. Brush the pork chops with oil and rub with spice mixture.
3. Insert a crisper plate in the Ninja Foodi air fryer baskets.
4. Place the pork chops in both baskets.
5. Select zone 1, then select "bake" mode and set the temperature to 410 degrees F for 15 minutes. Press "match" to match zone 2 settings to zone 1. Press "start/stop" to begin. Turn halfway through.

Nutrition:
- (Per serving) Calories 394 | Fat 31.7g | Sodium 118mg | Carbs 0.2g | Fiber 0.1g | Sugar 0.1g | Protein 25.5g

Steaks With Walnut-blue Cheese Butter

Servings: 6
Cooking Time: 10 Minutes
Ingredients:

- 120 ml unsalted butter, at room temperature
- 120 ml crumbled blue cheese
- 2 tablespoons finely chopped walnuts
- 1 tablespoon minced fresh rosemary
- 1 teaspoon minced garlic
- ¼ teaspoon cayenne pepper
- Sea salt and freshly ground black pepper, to taste
- 680 g sirloin steaks, at room temperature

Directions:
1. In a medium bowl, combine the butter, blue cheese, walnuts, rosemary, garlic, and cayenne pepper and salt and black pepper to taste. Use clean hands to ensure that everything is well combined. Place the mixture on a sheet of parchment paper and form it into a log. Wrap it tightly in plastic wrap. Refrigerate for at least 2 hours or freeze for 30 minutes.
2. Season the steaks generously with salt and pepper.
3. Set the air fryer to 204°C and let it preheat for 5 minutes.
4. Place the steaks in the two drawers in a single layer and air fry for 5 minutes. Flip the steaks, and cook for 5 minutes more, until an instant-read thermometer reads 49°C for medium-rare .
5. Transfer the steaks to a plate. Cut the butter into pieces and place the desired amount on top of the steaks. Tent a piece of aluminum foil over the steaks and allow to sit for 10 minutes before serving.
6. Store any remaining butter in a sealed container in the refrigerator for up to 2 weeks.

Garlic Sirloin Steak

Servings: 4
Cooking Time: 10 Minutes
Ingredients:

- 4 sirloin steak
- 30ml olive oil
- 28g steak sauce
- ½ tsp ground coriander
- 1 tsp garlic, minced
- 1 tbsp thyme, chopped
- Pepper
- Salt

Directions:
1. In a bowl, mix steak with thyme, oil, steak sauce, coriander, garlic, pepper, and salt. Cover and set aside for 2 hours.
2. Insert a crisper plate in Ninja Foodi air fryer baskets.
3. Place the marinated steaks in both baskets.
4. Select zone 1 then select air fry mode and set the temperature to 360 degrees F for 10 minutes. Press "match" and then "start/stop" to begin.

Nutrition:
- (Per serving) Calories 348 | Fat 18.1g |Sodium 39mg | Carbs 0.7g | Fiber 0.3g | Sugar 0g | Protein 0.1g

Tasty Pork Skewers

Servings: 3
Cooking Time: 10 Minutes
Ingredients:

- 450g pork shoulder, cut into ¼-inch pieces
- 66ml soy sauce
- ½ tbsp garlic, crushed
- 1 tbsp ginger paste
- 1 ½ tsp sesame oil
- 22ml rice vinegar
- 21ml honey
- Pepper
- Salt

Directions:
1. In a bowl, mix meat with the remaining ingredients. Cover and place in the refrigerator for 30 minutes.
2. Thread the marinated meat onto the soaked skewers.

3. Insert a crisper plate in the Ninja Foodi air fryer baskets.
4. Place the pork skewers in both baskets.
5. Select zone 1, then select "air fry" mode and set the temperature to 360 degrees F for 10 minutes. Press "match" and then press "start/stop" to begin. Turn halfway through.

Nutrition:
- (Per serving) Calories 520 | Fat 34.7g | Sodium 1507mg | Carbs 12.2g | Fiber 0.5g | Sugar 9.1g | Protein 37g

Mozzarella Stuffed Beef And Pork Meatballs

Servings: 4 To 6
Cooking Time: 12 Minutes

Ingredients:
- 1 tablespoon olive oil
- 1 small onion, finely chopped
- 1 to 2 cloves garlic, minced
- 340 g beef mince
- 340 g pork mince
- 180 ml bread crumbs
- 60 ml grated Parmesan cheese
- 60 ml finely chopped fresh parsley
- ½ teaspoon dried oregano
- 1½ teaspoons salt
- Freshly ground black pepper, to taste
- 2 eggs, lightly beaten
- 140 g low-moisture Mozzarella or other melting cheese, cut into 1-inch cubes

Directions:
1. Preheat a skillet over medium-high heat. Add the oil and cook the onion and garlic until tender, but not browned. 2. Transfer the onion and garlic to a large bowl and add the beef, pork, bread crumbs, Parmesan cheese, parsley, oregano, salt, pepper and eggs. Mix well until all the ingredients are combined. Divide the mixture into 12 evenly sized balls. Make one meatball at a time, by pressing a hole in the meatball mixture with the finger and pushing a piece of Mozzarella cheese into the hole. Mold the meat back into a ball, enclosing the cheese. 3. Preheat the air fryer to 192ºC. 4. Transfer meatballs to the two air fryer drawers and air fry for 12 minutes, shaking the drawers and turning the meatballs twice during the cooking process. Serve warm.

Rosemary And Garlic Lamb Chops

Servings: 4
Cooking Time: 15 Minutes

Ingredients:
- 8 lamb chops
- 3 tablespoons olive oil
- 2 tablespoons chopped fresh rosemary
- 1 teaspoon garlic powder or 3 cloves garlic, minced
- 1 teaspoon salt, or to taste
- ½ teaspoon black pepper, or to taste

Directions:
1. Dry the lamb chops with a paper towel.
2. Combine the olive oil, rosemary, garlic, salt, and pepper in a large mixing bowl. Toss the lamb in the marinade gently to coat it. Cover and set aside to marinate for 1 hour or up to overnight.
3. Install a crisper plate in both drawers. Place half the lamb chops in the zone 1 drawer and half in zone 2's, then insert the drawers into the unit.
4. Select zone 1, select AIR FRY, set temperature to 390 degrees F/ 200 degrees C, and set time to 15 minutes. Select MATCH to match zone 2 settings to zone 1. Press the START/STOP button to begin cooking.
5. When the time reaches 10 minutes, press START/STOP to pause the unit. Remove the drawers and flip the chops. Re-insert the drawers into the unit and press START/STOP to resume cooking.
6. Serve and enjoy!

Nutrition:
- (Per serving) Calories 427 | Fat 34g | Sodium 668mg | Carbs 1g | Fiber 1g | Sugar 1g | Protein 31g

Sweet And Spicy Country-style Ribs

Servings: 4
Cooking Time: 25 Minutes

Ingredients:

- 2 tablespoons brown sugar
- 2 tablespoons smoked paprika
- 1 teaspoon garlic powder
- 1 teaspoon onion granules
- 1 teaspoon mustard powder
- 1 teaspoon ground cumin
- 1 teaspoon coarse or flaky salt
- 1 teaspoon black pepper
- ¼ to ½ teaspoon cayenne pepper
- 680 g boneless pork steaks
- 235 ml barbecue sauce

Directions:

1. In a small bowl, stir together the brown sugar, paprika, garlic powder, onion granules, mustard powder, cumin, salt, black pepper, and cayenne. Mix until well combined.
2. Pat the ribs dry with a paper towel. Generously sprinkle the rub evenly over both sides of the ribs and rub in with your fingers.
3. Place the ribs in the two air fryer drawers. Set the air fryer to 176°C for 15 minutes. Turn the ribs and brush with 120 ml of the barbecue sauce. Cook for an additional 10 minutes. Use a meat thermometer to ensure the pork has reached an internal temperature of 64°C.
4. Serve with remaining barbecue sauce.

Roasted Beef

Servings: 8
Cooking Time: 50 Minutes

Ingredients:

- 1 (1-pound) beef roast
- Salt and ground black pepper, as required

Directions:

1. Grease each basket of "Zone 1" and "Zone 2" of Ninja Foodi 2-Basket Air Fryer.
2. Press "Zone 1" and "Zone 2" and then rotate the knob for each zone to select "Roast".
3. Set the temperature to 350 degrees F/ 175 degrees C for both zones and then set the time for 5 minutes to preheat.
4. Rub ach roast with salt and black pepper generously.
5. After preheating, arrange the roast into the basket of each zone.
6. Slide each basket into Air Fryer and set the time for 50 minutes.
7. After cooking time is completed, remove each roast from Air Fryer and place onto a platter for about 10 minutes before slicing.
8. With a sharp knife, cut each roast into desired-sized slices and serve.

Bo Luc Lac

Servings: 4
Cooking Time: 8 Minutes

Ingredients:

- For the Meat:
- 2 teaspoons soy sauce
- 4 garlic cloves, minced
- 1 teaspoon coarse or flaky salt
- 2 teaspoons sugar
- ¼ teaspoon ground black pepper
- 1 teaspoon toasted sesame oil
- 680 g top rump steak, cut into 1-inch cubes
- Cooking spray
- For the Salad:
- 1 head butterhead lettuce, leaves separated and torn into large pieces
- 60 ml fresh mint leaves
- 120 ml halved baby plum tomatoes
- ½ red onion, halved and thinly sliced
- 2 tablespoons apple cider vinegar
- 1 garlic clove, minced
- 2 teaspoons sugar
- ¼ teaspoon coarse or flaky salt
- ¼ teaspoon ground black pepper

- 2 tablespoons vegetable oil
- For Serving:
- Lime wedges, for garnish
- Coarse salt and freshly cracked black pepper, to taste

Directions:
1. Combine the ingredients for the meat, except for the steak, in a large bowl. Stir to mix well.
2. Dunk the steak cubes in the bowl and press to coat. Wrap the bowl in plastic and marinate under room temperature for at least 30 minutes.
3. Preheat the air fryer to 232°C. Spritz the two air fryer drawers with cooking spray.
4. Discard the marinade and transfer the steak cubes in the two preheated air fryer drawers.
5. Air fry for 4 minutes or until the steak cubes are lightly browned but still have a little pink. Shake the drawers halfway through the cooking time.
6. Meanwhile, combine the ingredients for the salad in a separate large bowl. Toss to mix well.
7. Pour the salad in a large serving bowl and top with the steak cubes. Squeeze the lime wedges over and sprinkle with salt and black pepper before serving.

Blue Cheese Steak Salad

Servings: 4
Cooking Time: 22 Minutes
Ingredients:
- 2 tablespoons balsamic vinegar
- 2 tablespoons red wine vinegar
- 1 tablespoon Dijon mustard
- 1 tablespoon granulated sweetener
- 1 teaspoon minced garlic
- Sea salt and freshly ground black pepper, to taste
- 180 ml extra-virgin olive oil
- 450 g boneless rump steak
- Avocado oil spray
- 1 small red onion, cut into ¼-inch-thick rounds
- 170 g baby spinach
- 120 ml cherry tomatoes, halved
- 85 g blue cheese, crumbled

Directions:
1. In a blender, combine the balsamic vinegar, red wine vinegar, Dijon mustard, sweetener, and garlic. Season with salt and pepper and process until smooth. With the blender running, drizzle in the olive oil. Process until well combined. Transfer to a jar with a tight-fitting lid, and refrigerate until ready to serve.
2. Season the steak with salt and pepper and let sit at room temperature for at least 45 minutes, time permitting.
3. Set the zone 1 air fryer drawer to 204°C. Spray the steak with oil and place it in the zone 1 air fryer drawer. Spray the onion slices with oil and place them in the zone 2 air fryer drawer.
4. In zone 1, air fry for 6 minutes. Flip the steak and spray it with more oil. Air fry for 6 minutes more for medium-rare or until the steak is done to your liking.
5. In zone 2, cook at 204°C for 5 minutes. Flip the onion slices and spray them with more oil. Air fry for 5 minutes more.
6. Transfer the steak to a plate, tent with a piece of aluminum foil, and allow it to rest. Slice the steak diagonally into thin strips. Place the spinach, cherry tomatoes, onion slices, and steak in a large bowl. Toss with the desired amount of dressing. Sprinkle with crumbled blue cheese and serve.

Bacon Wrapped Pork Tenderloin

Servings: 2
Cooking Time: 20 Minutes
Ingredients:
- ½ teaspoon salt
- ¼ teaspoon black pepper
- 1 pork tenderloin
- 6 center cut strips bacon
- cooking string

Directions:
1. Cut two bacon strips in half and place them on the working surface.
2. Place the other bacon strips on top and lay the tenderloin over the bacon strip.
3. Wrap the bacon around the tenderloin and tie the roast with a kitchen string.

4. Place the roast in the first air fryer basket.
5. Return the air fryer basket 1 to Zone 1, and basket 2 to Zone 2 of the Ninja Foodi 2-Basket Air Fryer.
6. Choose the "Air Fry" mode for Zone 1 and set the temperature to 400 degrees F and 20 minutes of cooking time.
7. Initiate cooking by pressing the START/PAUSE BUTTON.
8. Slice and serve warm.

Nutrition:
- (Per serving) Calories 459 | Fat 17.7g |Sodium 1516mg | Carbs 1.7g | Fiber 0.5g | Sugar 0.4g | Protein 69.2g

Roast Souvlaki-style Pork With Lemon-feta Baby Potatoes

Servings:4
Cooking Time: 40 Minutes

Ingredients:
- FOR THE PORK
- 1½ pounds pork tenderloin, cut into bite-size cubes
- ¼ cup olive oil
- ¼ cup fresh lemon juice
- 2 teaspoons minced garlic
- 2 teaspoons honey
- 1½ teaspoons dried oregano
- ¼ teaspoon kosher salt
- ¼ teaspoon freshly ground black pepper
- FOR THE POTATOES
- 1 pound baby red or yellow potatoes, halved
- 1 tablespoon olive oil
- Grated zest and juice of 1 lemon
- ½ teaspoon kosher salt
- ¼ teaspoon freshly ground black pepper
- ⅓ cup crumbled feta cheese
- 2 tablespoons chopped fresh parsley

Directions:
1. To prep the pork: In a large bowl, combine the pork, oil, lemon juice, garlic, honey, oregano, salt, and black pepper. If desired, cover and refrigerate up to 24 hours.
2. To prep the potatoes: In a large bowl, combine the potatoes, oil, lemon zest, lemon juice, salt, and black pepper. Mix to coat the potatoes.
3. To cook the pork and potatoes: Install a crisper plate in each of the two baskets. Place the pork in the Zone 1 basket and insert the basket in the unit. Place the potatoes in the Zone 2 basket and insert the basket in the unit.
4. Select Zone 1, select ROAST, set the temperature to 390°F, and set the time to 20 minutes.
5. Select Zone 2, select AIR FRY, set the temperature to 400°F, and set the time to 40 minutes. Select SMART FINISH.
6. Press START/PAUSE to begin cooking.
7. When cooking is complete, the pork will be cooked through (an instant-read thermometer should read 145°F) and the potatoes will be tender and beginning to brown around the edges.
8. Stir the feta and parsley into the potatoes. Serve the pork and potatoes while hot.

Nutrition:
- (Per serving) Calories: 395; Total fat: 17g; Saturated fat: 4.5g; Carbohydrates: 24g; Fiber: 2g; Protein: 37g; Sodium: 399mg

Chapter 7: Poultry Recipes

Chicken With Pineapple And Peach

Servings: 4
Cooking Time: 14 To 15 Minutes
Ingredients:

- 1 (450 g) low-sodium boneless, skinless chicken breasts, cut into 1-inch pieces
- 1 medium red onion, chopped
- 1 (230 g) can pineapple chunks, drained, 60 ml juice reserved
- 1 tablespoon peanut oil or safflower oil
- 1 peach, peeled, pitted, and cubed
- 1 tablespoon cornflour
- ½ teaspoon ground ginger
- ¼ teaspoon ground allspice
- Brown rice, cooked (optional)

Directions:
1. Preheat the air fryer to 195ºC.
2. In a medium metal bowl, mix the chicken, red onion, pineapple, and peanut oil. Bake in the air fryer for 9 minutes. Remove and stir.
3. Add the peach and return the bowl to the air fryer. Bake for 3 minutes more. Remove and stir again.
4. In a small bowl, whisk the reserved pineapple juice, the cornflour, ginger, and allspice well. Add to the chicken mixture and stir to combine.
5. Bake for 2 to 3 minutes more, or until the chicken reaches an internal temperature of 75ºC on a meat thermometer and the sauce is slightly thickened.
6. Serve immediately over hot cooked brown rice, if desired.

Chicken Caprese

Servings: 4
Cooking Time: 10 Minutes
Ingredients:

- 4 chicken breast cutlets
- 1 teaspoon Italian seasoning
- 1 teaspoon salt
- ½ teaspoon black pepper
- 4 slices fresh mozzarella cheese
- 1 large tomato, sliced
- Basil and balsamic vinegar to garnish

Directions:
1. Pat dry the chicken cutlets with a kitchen towel.
2. Rub the chicken with Italian seasoning, black pepper and salt.
3. Place two chicken breasts in each air fryer basket.
4. Return the air fryer basket 1 to Zone 1, and basket 2 to Zone 2 of the Ninja Foodi 2-Basket Air Fryer.
5. Choose the "Air Fry" mode for Zone 1 at 375 degrees F and 10 minutes of cooking time.
6. Select the "MATCH COOK" option to copy the settings for Zone 2.
7. Initiate cooking by pressing the START/PAUSE BUTTON.
8. After 10 minutes top each chicken breast with a slice of cheese and tomato slices.
9. Return the baskets to the Ninja Foodi 2 Baskets Air Fryer and air fry for 5 another minutes.
10. Garnish with balsamic vinegar and basil.
11. Serve warm.

Nutrition:

- (Per serving) Calories 502 | Fat 25g | Sodium 230mg | Carbs 1.5g | Fiber 0.2g | Sugar 0.4g | Protein 64.1g

Chili Chicken Wings

Servings: 4
Cooking Time: 43 Minutes.
Ingredients:

- 8 chicken wings drumettes
- cooking spray
- ⅛ cup low-fat buttermilk
- ¼ cup almond flour

- McCormick Chicken Seasoning to taste
- Thai Chili Marinade
- 1 ½ tablespoons low-sodium soy sauce
- ½ teaspoon ginger, minced
- 1 ½ garlic cloves
- 1 green onion
- ½ teaspoon rice wine vinegar
- ½ tablespoon Sriracha sauce
- ½ tablespoon sesame oil

Directions:
1. Put all the ingredients for the marinade in the blender and blend them for 1 minute.
2. Keep this marinade aside. Pat dry the washed chicken and place it in the Ziploc bag.
3. Add buttermilk, chicken seasoning, and zip the bag.
4. Shake the bag well, then refrigerator for 30 minutes for marination.
5. Remove the chicken drumettes from the marinade, then dredge them through dry flour.
6. Spread the drumettes in the two crisper plate and spray them with cooking oil.
7. Return the crisper plate to the Ninja Foodi Dual Zone Air Fryer.
8. Choose the Air Fry mode for Zone 1 and set the temperature to 390 degrees F and the time to 43 minutes.
9. Select the "MATCH" button to copy the settings for Zone 2.
10. Initiate cooking by pressing the START/STOP button.
11. Toss the drumettes once cooked halfway through.
12. Now brush the chicken pieces with Thai chili sauce and then resume cooking.
13. Serve warm.

Nutrition:
- (Per serving) Calories 223 | Fat 11.7g | Sodium 721mg | Carbs 13.6g | Fiber 0.7g | Sugar 8g | Protein 15.7g

Apricot-glazed Turkey Tenderloin

Servings: 4
Cooking Time: 30 Minutes

Ingredients:
- Olive oil
- 80 g sugar-free apricot preserves
- ½ tablespoon spicy brown mustard
- 680 g turkey breast tenderloin
- Salt and freshly ground black pepper, to taste

Directions:
1. Spray the two air fryer drawers lightly with olive oil.
2. In a small bowl, combine the apricot preserves and mustard to make a paste.
3. Season the turkey with salt and pepper. Spread the apricot paste all over the turkey.
4. Place the turkey in the two air fryer drawers and lightly spray with olive oil.
5. Air fry at 190°C for 15 minutes. Flip the turkey over and lightly spray with olive oil. Air fry until the internal temperature reaches at least 80°C, an additional 10 to 15 minutes.
6. Let the turkey rest for 10 minutes before slicing and serving.

Almond Chicken

Servings: 4
Cooking Time: 25 Minutes

Ingredients:
- 2 large eggs
- ½ cup buttermilk
- 2 teaspoons garlic salt
- 1 teaspoon pepper
- 2 cups slivered almonds, finely chopped
- 4 boneless, skinless chicken breast halves (6 ounces each)

Directions:
1. Whisk together the egg, buttermilk, garlic salt, and pepper in a small bowl.
2. In another small bowl, place the almonds.
3. Dip the chicken in the egg mixture, then roll it in the almonds, patting it down to help the coating stick.

4. Install a crisper plate in both drawers. Place half the chicken breasts in the zone 1 drawer and half in zone 2's, then insert the drawers into the unit.
5. Select zone 1, select AIR FRY, set temperature to 390 degrees F/ 200 degrees C, and set time to 22 minutes. Select MATCH to match zone 2 settings to zone 1. Press the START/STOP button to begin cooking.
6. When the time reaches 11 minutes, press START/STOP to pause the unit. Remove the drawers and flip the chicken. Re-insert the drawers into the unit and press START/STOP to resume cooking.
7. When cooking is complete, remove the chicken.

Nutrition:
- (Per serving) Calories 353 | Fat 18g | Sodium 230mg | Carbs 6g | Fiber 2g | Sugar 3g | Protein 41g

Sweet And Spicy Carrots With Chicken Thighs

Servings: 2
Cooking Time: 35

Ingredients:
- Cooking spray, for greasing
- 2 tablespoons butter, melted
- 1 tablespoon hot honey
- 1 teaspoon orange zest
- 1 teaspoon cardamom
- ½ pound baby carrots
- 1 tablespoon orange juice
- Salt and black pepper, to taste
- ½ pound of carrots, baby carrots
- 8 chicken thighs

Directions:
1. Take a bowl and mix all the glaze ingredients in it.
2. Now, coat the chicken and carrots with the glaze and let it rest for 30 minutes.
3. Now place the chicken thighs into the zone 1 basket.
4. Next put the glazed carrots into the zone 2 basket.
5. Press button 1 for the first basket and set it to ROAST Mode at 350 degrees F for 35 minutes.
6. For the second basket hit 2 and set time to AIRFRY mode at 390 degrees F for 8-10 minutes.
7. Once the cooking cycle completes take out the carrots and chicken and serve it hot.

Nutrition:
- (Per serving) Calories 1312| Fat 55.4g| Sodium 757mg | Carbs 23.3g | Fiber6.7 g | Sugar12 g | Protein171 g

Garlic Parmesan Drumsticks

Servings: 4
Cooking Time: 25 Minutes

Ingredients:
- 8 (115 g) chicken drumsticks
- ½ teaspoon salt
- ⅛ teaspoon ground black pepper
- ½ teaspoon garlic powder
- 2 tablespoons salted butter, melted
- 45 g grated Parmesan cheese
- 1 tablespoon dried parsley

Directions:
1. Sprinkle drumsticks with salt, pepper, and garlic powder. Place drumsticks into the two ungreased air fryer baskets.
2. Adjust the temperature to 200ºC and air fry for 25 minutes, turning drumsticks halfway through cooking. Drumsticks will be golden and have an internal temperature of at least 75ºC when done.
3. Transfer drumsticks to a large serving dish. Pour butter over drumsticks, and sprinkle with Parmesan and parsley. Serve warm.

Roasted Garlic Chicken Pizza With Cauliflower "wings"

Servings: 4
Cooking Time: 25 Minutes

Ingredients:
- FOR THE PIZZA
- 2 prebaked rectangular pizza crusts or flatbreads
- 2 tablespoons olive oil
- 1 tablespoon minced garlic

- 1½ cups shredded part-skim mozzarella cheese
- 6 ounces boneless, skinless chicken breast, thinly sliced
- ¼ teaspoon red pepper flakes (optional)
- FOR THE CAULIFLOWER "WINGS"
- 4 cups cauliflower florets
- 1 tablespoon vegetable oil
- ½ cup Buffalo wing sauce

Directions:
1. To prep the pizza: Trim the pizza crusts to fit in the air fryer basket, if necessary.
2. Brush the top of each crust with the oil and sprinkle with the garlic. Top the crusts with the mozzarella, chicken, and red pepper flakes (if using).
3. To prep the cauliflower "wings": In a large bowl, combine the cauliflower and oil and toss to coat the florets.
4. To cook the pizza and "wings": Install a crisper plate in each of the two baskets. Place one pizza in the Zone 1 basket and insert the basket in the unit. Place the cauliflower in the Zone 2 basket and insert the basket in the unit.
5. Select Zone 1, select ROAST, set the temperature to 375°F, and set the time to 25 minutes.
6. Select Zone 2, select AIR FRY, set the temperature to 390°F, and set the time to 25 minutes. Select SMART FINISH.
7. Press START/PAUSE to begin cooking.
8. When the Zone 1 timer reads 13 minutes, press START/PAUSE. Remove the basket. Transfer the pizza to a cutting board (the chicken should be cooked through and the cheese melted and bubbling). Add the second pizza to the basket. Reinsert the basket in the unit and press START/PAUSE to resume cooking.
9. When the Zone 2 timer reads 5 minutes, press START/PAUSE. Remove the basket and add the Buffalo wing sauce to the cauliflower. Shake well to evenly coat the cauliflower in the sauce. Reinsert the basket and press START/PAUSE to resume cooking.
10. When cooking is complete, the cauliflower will be crisp on the outside and tender inside, and the chicken on the second pizza will be cooked through and the cheese melted.
11. Cut each pizza into 4 slices. Serve with the cauliflower "wings" on the side.

Nutrition:
- (Per serving) Calories: 360; Total fat: 20g; Saturated fat: 6.5g; Carbohydrates: 21g; Fiber: 2.5g; Protein: 24g; Sodium: 1,399mg

Turkey Meatloaf With Veggie Medley

Servings:4
Cooking Time: 30 Minutes

Ingredients:
- FOR THE MEATLOAF
- 1 large egg
- ¼ cup ketchup
- 2 teaspoons Worcestershire sauce
- ½ cup Italian-style bread crumbs
- 1 teaspoon kosher salt
- 1 pound ground turkey (93 percent lean)
- 1 tablespoon vegetable oil
- FOR THE VEGGIE MEDLEY
- 2 carrots, thinly sliced
- 8 ounces green beans, trimmed (about 2 cups)
- 2 cups broccoli florets
- 1 red bell pepper, sliced into strips
- 2 tablespoons vegetable oil
- ½ teaspoon kosher salt
- ½ teaspoon freshly ground black pepper

Directions:
1. To prep the meatloaf: In a large bowl, whisk the egg. Stir in the ketchup, Worcestershire sauce, bread crumbs, and salt. Let sit for 5 minutes to allow the bread crumbs to absorb some moisture.
2. Gently mix in the turkey until just incorporated. Form the mixture into a loaf. Brush with the oil.
3. To prep the veggie medley: In a large bowl, combine the carrots, green beans, broccoli, bell pepper, oil, salt, and black pepper. Mix well to coat the vegetables with the oil.
4. To cook the meatloaf and veggie medley: Install a crisper plate in each of the two baskets. Place the meatloaf in the Zone 1 basket and insert the basket in the unit. Place the vegetables in the Zone 2 basket and insert the basket in the unit.
5. Select Zone 1, select ROAST, set the temperature to 350°F, and set the time to 30 minutes.

6. Select Zone 2, select AIR FRY, set the temperature to 390°F, and set the time to 20 minutes. Select SMART FINISH.
7. Press START/PAUSE to begin cooking.
8. When cooking is complete, the meatloaf will be cooked through (an instant-read thermometer should read 165°F) and the vegetables will be tender and roasted.

Nutrition:
- (Per serving) Calories: 394; Total fat: 20g; Saturated fat: 4.5g; Carbohydrates: 25g; Fiber: 4.5g; Protein: 28g; Sodium: 952mg

Pretzel Chicken Cordon Bleu

Servings: 4
Cooking Time: 26 Minutes

Ingredients:
- 5 boneless chicken thighs
- 3 cups pretzels, crushed
- 2 eggs, beaten
- 10 deli honey ham, slices
- 5 Swiss cheese slices
- Cooking spray

Directions:
1. Grind pretzels in a food processor.
2. Pound the chicken tights with a mallet.
3. Top each chicken piece with one cheese slice and 2 ham slices.
4. Roll the chicken pieces and secure with a toothpick.
5. Dip the rolls in the eggs and coat with the breadcrumbs.
6. Place these rolls in the air fryer baskets.
7. Spray them with cooking oil.
8. Return the air fryer basket 1 to Zone 1, and basket 2 to Zone 2 of the Ninja Foodi 2-Basket Air Fryer.
9. Choose the "Air Fry" mode for Zone 1 and set the temperature to 375 degrees F and 26 minutes of cooking time.
10. Select the "MATCH COOK" option to copy the settings for Zone 2.
11. Initiate cooking by pressing the START/PAUSE BUTTON.
12. Flip the rolls once cooked halfway through.
13. Serve warm.

Nutrition:
- (Per serving) Calories 380 | Fat 29g | Sodium 821mg | Carbs 34.6g | Fiber 0g | Sugar 0g | Protein 30g

Crispy Dill Chicken Strips

Servings: 4
Cooking Time: 10 Minutes

Ingredients:
- 2 whole boneless, skinless chicken breasts (about 450 g each), halved lengthwise
- 230 ml Italian dressing
- 110 g finely crushed crisps
- 1 tablespoon dried dill weed
- 1 tablespoon garlic powder
- 1 large egg, beaten
- 1 to 2 tablespoons oil

Directions:
1. In a large resealable bag, combine the chicken and Italian dressing. Seal the bag and refrigerate to marinate at least 1 hour.
2. In a shallow dish, stir together the potato chips, dill, and garlic powder. Place the beaten egg in a second shallow dish.
3. Remove the chicken from the marinade. Roll the chicken pieces in the egg and the crisp mixture, coating thoroughly.
4. Preheat the air fryer to 170°C. Line the two air fryer drawers with parchment paper.
5. Place the coated chicken on the parchment and spritz with oil.
6. Cook for 5 minutes. Flip the chicken, spritz it with oil, and cook for 5 minutes more until the outsides are crispy and the insides are no longer pink.

Stuffed Chicken Florentine

Servings: 4
Cooking Time: 20 Minutes
Ingredients:
- 3 tablespoons pine nuts
- 40 g frozen spinach, thawed and squeezed dry
- 75 g ricotta cheese
- 2 tablespoons grated Parmesan cheese
- 3 cloves garlic, minced
- Salt and freshly ground black pepper, to taste
- 4 small boneless, skinless chicken breast halves (about 680 g)
- 8 slices bacon

Directions:
1. In a large bowl, combine the spinach, ricotta, Parmesan, and garlic. Season to taste with salt and pepper and stir well until thoroughly combined.
2. Using a sharp knife, cut into the chicken breasts, slicing them across and opening them up like a book, but be careful not to cut them all the way through. Sprinkle the chicken with salt and pepper.
3. Spoon equal amounts of the spinach mixture into the chicken, then fold the top of the chicken breast back over the top of the stuffing. Wrap each chicken breast with 2 slices of bacon.
4. Air fry the chicken for 18 to 20 minutes in zone 1 drawer until the bacon is crisp and a thermometer inserted into the thickest part of the chicken registers 76ºC.
5. Place the pine nuts in a small pan and set in the zone 2 air fryer drawer. Air fry at 200ºC for 2 to 3 minutes until toasted. Remove the pine nuts to a mixing bowl.

Chicken With Bacon And Tomato & Bacon-wrapped Stuffed Chicken Breasts

Servings: 8
Cooking Time: 30 Minutes
Ingredients:
- Chicken with Bacon and Tomato:
- 4 medium-sized skin-on chicken drumsticks
- 1½ teaspoons herbs de Provence
- Salt and pepper, to taste
- 1 tablespoon rice vinegar
- 2 tablespoons olive oil
- 2 garlic cloves, crushed
- 340 g crushed canned tomatoes
- 1 small-size leek, thinly sliced
- 2 slices smoked bacon, chopped
- Bacon-Wrapped Stuffed Chicken Breasts:
- 80 g chopped frozen spinach, thawed and squeezed dry
- 55 g cream cheese, softened
- 20 g grated Parmesan cheese
- 1 jalapeño, seeded and chopped
- ½ teaspoon kosher salt
- 1 teaspoon black pepper
- 2 large boneless, skinless chicken breasts, butterflied and pounded to ½-inch thickness
- 4 teaspoons salt-free Cajun seasoning
- 6 slices bacon

Directions:
1. Make the Chicken with Bacon and Tomato :
2. Sprinkle the chicken drumsticks with herbs de Provence, salt and pepper; then, drizzle them with rice vinegar and olive oil.
3. Place into a baking pan and cook in the zone 1 basket at 180ºC for 8 to 10 minutes. Pause the air fryer; stir in the remaining ingredients and continue to cook for 15 minutes longer; make sure to check them periodically. Bon appétit!
4. Make the Bacon-Wrapped Stuffed Chicken Breasts :
5. In a small bowl, combine the spinach, cream cheese, Parmesan cheese, jalapeño, salt, and pepper. Stir until well combined.
6. Place the butterflied chicken breasts on a flat surface. Spread the cream cheese mixture evenly across each piece of chicken. Starting with the narrow end, roll up each chicken breast, ensuring the filling stays inside. Season chicken with the Cajun seasoning, patting it in to ensure it sticks to the meat.
7. Wrap each breast in 3 slices of bacon. Place in the zone 2 air fryer basket. Set the air fryer to 180ºC for 30 minutes. Use a meat thermometer to ensure the chicken has reached an internal temperature of 75ºC.
8. Let the chicken stand 5 minutes before slicing each rolled-up breast in half to serve.

Juicy Duck Breast

Servings: 1
Cooking Time: 20 Minutes
Ingredients:
- ½ duck breast
- Salt and black pepper, to taste
- 2 tablespoons plum sauce

Directions:
1. Rub the duck breast with black pepper and salt.
2. Place the duck breast in air fryer basket 1 and add plum sauce on top.
3. Return the basket to the Ninja Foodi 2 Baskets Air Fryer.
4. Choose the "Air Fry" mode for Zone 1 and set the temperature to 400 degrees F and 20 minutes of cooking time.
5. Initiate cooking by pressing the START/PAUSE BUTTON.
6. Flip the duck breast once cooked halfway through.
7. Serve warm.

Nutrition:
- (Per serving) Calories 379 | Fat 19g | Sodium 184mg | Carbs 12.3g | Fiber 0.6g | Sugar 2g | Protein 37.7g

Chicken And Vegetable Fajitas

Servings: 6
Cooking Time: 23 Minutes
Ingredients:
- Chicken:
- 450 g boneless, skinless chicken thighs, cut crosswise into thirds
- 1 tablespoon vegetable oil
- 4½ teaspoons taco seasoning
- Vegetables:
- 50 g sliced onion
- 150 g sliced bell pepper
- 1 or 2 jalapeños, quartered lengthwise
- 1 tablespoon vegetable oil
- ½ teaspoon kosher salt
- ½ teaspoon ground cumin
- For Serving:
- Tortillas
- Sour cream
- Shredded cheese
- Guacamole
- Salsa

Directions:
1. For the chicken: In a medium bowl, toss together the chicken, vegetable oil, and taco seasoning to coat. 2. For the vegetables: In a separate bowl, toss together the onion, bell pepper, jalapeño, vegetable oil, salt, and cumin to coat. 3. Place the chicken in the air fryer basket. Set the air fryer to (190ºC for 10 minutes. Add the vegetables to the basket, toss everything together to blend the seasonings, and set the air fryer for 13 minutes more. Use a meat thermometer to ensure the chicken has reached an internal temperature of 75ºC. 4. Transfer the chicken and vegetables to a serving platter. Serve with tortillas and the desired fajita fixings.

Curried Orange Honey Chicken

Servings: 4
Cooking Time: 16 To 19 Minutes
Ingredients:
- 340 g boneless, skinless chicken thighs, cut into 1-inch pieces
- 1 yellow bell pepper, cut into 1½-inch pieces
- 1 small red onion, sliced
- Olive oil for misting
- 60 ml chicken stock
- 2 tablespoons honey
- 60 ml orange juice
- 1 tablespoon cornflour
- 2 to 3 teaspoons curry powder

Directions:
1. Preheat the air fryer to 190ºC.
2. Put the chicken thighs, pepper, and red onion in the zone 1 air fryer drawer and mist with olive oil.

3. Roast for 12 to 14 minutes or until the chicken is cooked to 76ºC, shaking the drawer halfway through cooking time.
4. Remove the chicken and vegetables from the air fryer drawer and set aside.
5. In a metal bowl, combine the stock, honey, orange juice, cornflour, and curry powder, and mix well. Add the chicken and vegetables, stir, and put the bowl in the drawer.
6. Return the drawer to the air fryer and roast for 2 minutes. Remove and stir, then roast for 2 to 3 minutes or until the sauce is thickened and bubbly.
7. Serve warm.

Air Fried Chicken Potatoes With Sun-dried Tomato

Servings: 2
Cooking Time: 25 Minutes

Ingredients:
- 2 teaspoons minced fresh oregano, divided
- 2 teaspoons minced fresh thyme, divided
- 2 teaspoons extra-virgin olive oil, plus extra as needed
- 450 g fingerling potatoes, unpeeled
- 2 (340 g) bone-in split chicken breasts, trimmed
- 1 garlic clove, minced
- 15 g oil-packed sun-dried tomatoes, patted dry and chopped
- 1½ tablespoons red wine vinegar
- 1 tablespoon capers, rinsed and minced
- 1 small shallot, minced
- Salt and ground black pepper, to taste

Directions:
1. Preheat the zone 1 air fryer drawer to 180ºC.
2. Combine 1 teaspoon of oregano, 1 teaspoon of thyme, ¼ teaspoon of salt, ¼ teaspoon of ground black pepper, 1 teaspoons of olive oil in a large bowl. Add the potatoes and toss to coat well.
3. Combine the chicken with remaining thyme, oregano, and olive oil. Sprinkle with garlic, salt, and pepper. Toss to coat well.
4. Place the potatoes in the preheated air fryer drawer, then arrange the chicken on top of the potatoes.
5. Air fry for 25 minutes or until the internal temperature of the chicken reaches at least 76ºC and the potatoes are wilted. Flip the chicken and potatoes halfway through.
6. Meanwhile, combine the sun-dried tomatoes, vinegar, capers, and shallot in a separate large bowl. Sprinkle with salt and ground black pepper. Toss to mix well.
7. Remove the chicken and potatoes from the air fryer and allow to cool for 10 minutes. Serve with the sun-dried tomato mix.

Spiced Chicken And Vegetables

Servings:1
Cooking Time:45

Ingredients:
- 2 large chicken breasts
- 2 teaspoons of olive oil
- 1 teaspoon of chili powder
- 1 teaspoon of paprika powder
- 1 teaspoon of onion powder
- ½ teaspoon of garlic powder
- 1/4 teaspoon of Cumin
- Salt and black pepper, to taste
- Vegetable Ingredients:
- 2 large potato, cubed
- 4 large carrots cut into bite-size pieces
- 1 tablespoon of olive oil
- Salt and black pepper, to taste

Directions:
1. Take chicken breast pieces and rub olive oil, salt, pepper, chili powder, onion powder, cumin, garlic powder, and paprika.
2. Season the vegetables with olive oil, salt, and black pepper.
3. Now put the chicken breast pieces in the zone 1 basket.
4. Put the vegetables into the zone 2 basket.

5. Now hit 1 for the first basket and set it to ROAST at 350 degrees F, for 45 minutes.
6. For the second basket hit 2 and set time for 45 minutes, by selecting AIR FRY mode at 350 degrees F.
7. To start cooking hit the smart finish button and press hit start.
8. Once the cooking cycle is done, serve, and enjoy.

Nutrition:
- (Per serving) Calories1510 | Fat 51.3g| Sodium 525mg | Carbs 163g | Fiber24.7 g | Sugar 21.4g | Protein 102.9

Chicken Ranch Wraps

Servings: 4
Cooking Time: 22 Minutes

Ingredients:
- 1½ ounces breaded chicken breast tenders
- 4 (12-inch) whole-wheat tortilla wraps
- 2 heads romaine lettuce, chopped
- ½ cup shredded mozzarella cheese
- 4 tablespoons ranch dressing

Directions:
1. Place a crisper plate in each drawer. Place half of the chicken tenders in one drawer and half in the other. Insert the drawers into the unit.
2. Select zone 1, then AIR FRY, and set the temperature to 390 degrees F/ 200 degrees C with a 22-minute timer. To match zone 2 settings to zone 1, choose MATCH. To begin cooking, press the START/STOP button.
3. To pause the unit, press START/STOP when the timer reaches 11 minutes. Remove the drawers from the unit and flip the tenders over. To resume cooking, re-insert the drawers into the device and press START/STOP.
4. Remove the chicken from the drawers when they're done cooking and chop them up.
5. Divide the chopped chicken between warmed-up wraps. Top with some lettuce, cheese, and ranch dressing. Wrap and serve.

Nutrition:
- (Per serving) Calories 212 | Fat 7.8g | Sodium 567mg | Carbs 9.1g | Fiber 34.4g | Sugar 9.7g | Protein 10.6g

African Piri-piri Chicken Drumsticks

Servings: 2
Cooking Time: 20 Minutes

Ingredients:
- Chicken:
- 1 tablespoon chopped fresh thyme leaves
- 1 tablespoon minced fresh ginger
- 1 small shallot, finely chopped
- 2 garlic cloves, minced
- 80 ml piri-piri sauce or hot sauce
- 3 tablespoons extra-virgin olive oil
- Zest and juice of 1 lemon
- 1 teaspoon smoked paprika
- ½ teaspoon kosher salt
- ½ teaspoon black pepper
- 4 chicken drumsticks
- Glaze:
- 2 tablespoons butter or ghee
- 1 teaspoon chopped fresh thyme leaves
- 1 garlic clove, minced
- 1 tablespoon piri-piri sauce
- 1 tablespoon fresh lemon juice

Directions:
1. For the chicken: In a small bowl, stir together all the ingredients except the chicken. Place the chicken and the marinade in a gallon-size resealable plastic bag. Seal the bag and massage to coat. Refrigerate for at least 2 hours or up to 24 hours, turning the bag occasionally. 2. Place the chicken legs in the zone 1 air fryer basket. Set the air fryer to 200ºC for 20 minutes, turning the chicken halfway through the cooking time. 3. Meanwhile, for the glaze: Melt the butter in a small saucepan over medium-high heat. Add the thyme and garlic. Cook, stirring, until the garlic just begins to brown, 1 to 2 minutes. Add the piri-piri sauce and lemon juice. Reduce the heat to medium-low and simmer for 1 to 2 minutes. 4. Transfer the chicken to a serving platter. Pour the glaze over the chicken. Serve immediately.

Brazilian Chicken Drumsticks

Servings: 6
Cooking Time: 47 Minutes.

Ingredients:

- 2 teaspoons cumin seeds
- 2 teaspoons dried parsley
- 2 teaspoons turmeric powder
- 2 teaspoons dried oregano leaves
- 2 teaspoons salt
- 1 teaspoon coriander seeds
- 1 teaspoon black peppercorns
- 1 teaspoon cayenne pepper
- ½ cup lime juice
- 4 tablespoons vegetable oil
- 3 lbs. chicken drumsticks

Directions:

1. Grind cumin, parsley, salt, coriander seeds, cayenne pepper, peppercorns, oregano, and turmeric in a food processor.
2. Add this mixture to lemon juice and oil in a bowl and mix well.
3. Rub the spice paste over the chicken drumsticks and let them marinate for 30 minutes.
4. Divide the chicken drumsticks in both the crisper plates.
5. Return the crisper plates to the Ninja Foodi Dual Zone Air Fryer.
6. Choose the Air Fry mode for Zone 1 and set the temperature to 390 degrees F and the time to 47 minutes.
7. Select the "MATCH" button to copy the settings for Zone 2.
8. Initiate cooking by pressing the START/STOP button.
9. Flip the drumsticks when cooked halfway through, then resume cooking.
10. Serve warm.

Nutrition:

- (Per serving) Calories 456 | Fat 16.4g | Sodium 1321mg | Carbs 19.2g | Fiber 2.2g | Sugar 4.2g | Protein 55.2g

Wings With Corn On The Cob

Servings: 2
Cooking Time: 40 Minutes

Ingredients:

- 6 chicken wings, skinless
- 2 tablespoons coconut amino
- 2 tablespoons brown sugar
- 1 teaspoon ginger, paste
- ½ inch garlic, minced
- Salt and black pepper to taste
- 2 corn on cobs, small
- Oil spray, for greasing

Directions:

1. Spray the corns with oil spray and season them with salt.
2. Coat the chicken wings with coconut amino, brown sugar, ginger, garlic, salt, and black pepper.
3. Spray the wings with a good amount of oil spray.
4. Put the chicken wings in the zone 1 basket.
5. Put the corn into the zone 2 basket.
6. Select ROAST mode for the chicken wings and set the time to 23 minutes at 400 degrees F/ 200 degrees C.
7. Press 2 and select the AIR FRY mode for the corn and set the time to 40 at 300 degrees F/ 150 degrees C.
8. Once it's done, serve and enjoy.

Nutrition:

- (Per serving) Calories 950 | Fat 33.4g | Sodium 592 mg | Carbs 27.4g | Fiber 2.1g | Sugar 11.3 g | Protein 129g

Thai Curry Meatballs

Servings: 4
Cooking Time: 10 Minutes
Ingredients:
- 450 g chicken mince
- 15 g chopped fresh coriander
- 1 teaspoon chopped fresh mint
- 1 tablespoon fresh lime juice
- 1 tablespoon Thai red, green, or yellow curry paste
- 1 tablespoon fish sauce
- 2 garlic cloves, minced
- 2 teaspoons minced fresh ginger
- ½ teaspoon kosher salt
- ½ teaspoon black pepper
- ¼ teaspoon red pepper flakes

Directions:
1. Preheat the zone 1 air fryer drawer to 200°C.
2. In a large bowl, gently mix the chicken mince, coriander, mint, lime juice, curry paste, fish sauce, garlic, ginger, salt, black pepper, and red pepper flakes until thoroughly combined.
3. Form the mixture into 16 meatballs. Place the meatballs in a single layer in the zone 1 air fryer drawer. Air fry for 10 minutes, turning the meatballs halfway through the cooking time. Use a meat thermometer to ensure the meatballs have reached an internal temperature of 76°C. Serve immediately.

Cajun Chicken With Vegetables

Servings: 6
Cooking Time: 20 Minutes
Ingredients:
- 450g chicken breast, boneless & diced
- 1 tbsp Cajun seasoning
- 400g grape tomatoes
- ⅛ tsp dried thyme
- ⅛ tsp dried oregano
- 1 tsp smoked paprika
- 1 zucchini, diced
- 30ml olive oil
- 1 bell pepper, diced
- 1 tsp onion powder
- 1 ½ tsp garlic powder
- Pepper
- Salt

Directions:
1. In a bowl, toss chicken with vegetables, oil, herb, spices, and salt until well coated.
2. Insert a crisper plate in the Ninja Foodi air fryer baskets.
3. Add chicken and vegetable mixture to both baskets.
4. Select zone 1, then select "air fry" mode and set the temperature to 390 degrees F for 20 minutes. Press "match" to match zone 2 settings to zone 1. Press "start/stop" to begin.

Nutrition:
- (Per serving) Calories 153 | Fat 6.9g |Sodium 98mg | Carbs 6g | Fiber 1.6g | Sugar 3.5g | Protein 17.4g

Chicken Leg Piece

Servings:1
Cooking Time:25
Ingredients:
- 1 teaspoon of onion powder
- 1 teaspoon of paprika powder
- 1 teaspoon of garlic powder
- Salt and black pepper, to taste
- 1 tablespoon of Italian seasoning
- 1 teaspoon of celery seeds
- 2 eggs, whisked
- 1/3 cup buttermilk
- 1 cup of corn flour
- 1 pound of chicken leg

Directions:
1. Take a bowl and whisk egg along with pepper, salt, and buttermilk.
2. Set it aside for further use.

3. Mix all the spices in a small separate bowl.
4. Dredge the chicken in egg wash then dredge it in seasoning.
5. Coat the chicken legs with oil spray.
6. At the end dust it with the corn flour.
7. Divide the leg pieces into two zones.
8. Set zone 1 basket to 400 degrees F, for 25 minutes.
9. Select MATCH for zone 2 basket.
10. Let the air fryer do the magic.
11. Once it's done, serve and enjoy.

Nutrition:
- (Per serving) Calories 1511| Fat 52.3g| Sodium615 mg | Carbs 100g | Fiber 9.2g | Sugar 8.1g | Protein 154.2g

Garlic, Buffalo, And Blue Cheese Stuffed Chicken

Servings: 2
Cooking Time: 30 Minutes

Ingredients:
- ¼ teaspoon garlic powder
- ¼ teaspoon onion powder
- ¼ teaspoon paprika
- 2 boneless, skinless chicken breasts
- ½ tablespoon canola oil
- 2 ounces softened cream cheese
- ¼ cup shredded cheddar cheese
- ¼ cup blue cheese crumbles
- ¼ cup buffalo sauce
- 1 tablespoon dry ranch seasoning
- 2 tablespoons dried chives
- 1 tablespoon minced garlic
- Optional toppings:
- Ranch dressing
- Buffalo sauce
- Fresh parsley

Directions:
1. Combine the garlic powder, onion powder, and paprika in a small bowl.
2. Drizzle the chicken breasts with oil and season evenly with the garlic powder mixture on a cutting board.
3. Make a deep pocket in the center of each chicken breast, but be cautious not to cut all the way through.
4. Combine the remaining ingredients in a medium mixing bowl and stir until thoroughly blended. Fill each chicken breast's pocket with the cream cheese mixture.
5. Place the chicken in both drawers and insert both drawers into the unit. Select zone 1, then BAKE, and set the temperature to 375 degrees F/ 190 degrees C with a 30-minute timer. To match zone 2 and zone 1 settings, select MATCH. To start cooking, use the START/STOP button.
6. Garnish the cooked chicken with ranch dressing, spicy sauce, and parsley on top.

Nutrition:
- (Per serving) Calories 369 | Fat 23.8g | Sodium 568mg | Carbs 4.3g | Fiber 0.4g | Sugar 0.5g | Protein 34.7g

Asian Chicken Drumsticks

Servings: 4
Cooking Time: 20 Minutes

Ingredients:
- 8 chicken drumsticks
- 1 lime juice
- 30ml rice wine
- 45ml fish sauce
- 2 tbsp garlic, minced
- 55g brown sugar
- ½ tsp Sriracha sauce
- 1 tsp black pepper
- 1 tsp sesame oil
- Salt

Directions:
1. Add chicken drumsticks and remaining ingredients into the bowl and mix well. Cover and place in refrigerator for 4 hours.
2. Insert a crisper plate in the Ninja Foodi air fryer baskets.

3. Place the marinated chicken drumsticks in both baskets.
4. Select zone 1, then select "air fry" mode and set the temperature to 360 degrees F for 20 minutes. Press "match" to match zone 2 settings to zone 1. Press "start/stop" to begin.

Nutrition:
- (Per serving) Calories 225 | Fat 6.4g |Sodium 1223mg | Carbs 14.6g | Fiber 0.2g | Sugar 11.3g | Protein 26.3g

"fried" Chicken With Warm Baked Potato Salad

Servings:4
Cooking Time: 40 Minutes

Ingredients:
- FOR THE "FRIED" CHICKEN
- 1 cup buttermilk
- 1 tablespoon kosher salt
- 4 bone-in, skin-on chicken drumsticks and/or thighs
- 2 cups all-purpose flour
- 1 tablespoon seasoned salt
- 1 tablespoon paprika
- Nonstick cooking spray
- FOR THE POTATO SALAD
- 1½ pounds baby red potatoes, halved
- 1 tablespoon vegetable oil
- ½ cup mayonnaise
- ⅓ cup plain reduced-fat Greek yogurt
- 1 tablespoon apple cider vinegar
- ½ teaspoon kosher salt
- ½ teaspoon freshly ground black pepper
- ¾ cup shredded Cheddar cheese
- 4 slices cooked bacon, crumbled
- 3 scallions, sliced

Directions:
1. To prep the chicken: In a large bowl, combine the buttermilk and salt. Add the chicken and turn to coat. Let rest for at least 30 minutes (for the best flavor, marinate the chicken overnight in the refrigerator).
2. In a separate large bowl, combine the flour, seasoned salt, and paprika.
3. Remove the chicken from the marinade and allow any excess marinade to drip off. Discard the marinade. Dip the chicken pieces in the flour, coating them thoroughly. Mist with cooking spray. Let the chicken rest for 10 minutes.
4. To prep the potatoes: In a large bowl, combine the potatoes and oil and toss to coat.
5. To cook the chicken and potatoes: Install a crisper plate in the Zone 1 basket. Place the chicken in the basket in a single layer and insert the basket in the unit. Place the potatoes in the Zone 2 basket and insert the basket in the unit.
6. Select Zone 1, select AIR FRY, set the temperature to 390°F, and set the time to 30 minutes.
7. Select Zone 2, select BAKE, set the temperature to 400°F, and set the time to 40 minutes. Select SMART FINISH.
8. Press START/PAUSE to begin cooking.
9. When cooking is complete, the chicken will be golden brown and cooked through (an instant-read thermometer should read 165°F) and the potatoes will be fork-tender.
10. Rinse the potatoes under cold water for about 1 minute to cool them.
11. Place the potatoes in a large bowl and stir in the mayonnaise, yogurt, vinegar, salt, and black pepper. Gently stir in the Cheddar, bacon, and scallions. Serve warm with the "fried" chicken.

Nutrition:
- (Per serving) Calories: 639; Total fat: 38g; Saturated fat: 9.5g; Carbohydrates: 54g; Fiber: 4g; Protein: 21g; Sodium: 1,471mg

Asian Chicken

Servings: 4
Cooking Time: 12 Minutes

Ingredients:
- 8 chicken thighs, boneless
- 4 garlic cloves, minced
- 85g honey
- 120ml soy sauce
- 1 tsp dried oregano
- 2 tbsp parsley, chopped
- 1 tbsp ketchup

Directions:

1. Add chicken and remaining ingredients in a bowl and mix until well coated. Cover and place in the refrigerator for 6 hours.
2. Insert a crisper plate in the Ninja Foodi air fryer baskets.
3. Remove the chicken from the marinade and place them in both baskets.
4. Select zone 1 then select "air fry" mode and set the temperature to 390 degrees F for 12 minutes. Press "match" to match zone 2 settings to zone 1. Press "start/stop" to begin.

Nutrition:
- (Per serving) Calories 646 | Fat 21.7g |Sodium 2092mg | Carbs 22.2g | Fiber 0.6g | Sugar 18.9g | Protein 86.9g

Chicken Breast Strips

Servings:2
Cooking Time:22

Ingredients:
- 2 large organic egg
- 1-ounce buttermilk
- 1 cup of cornmeal
- ¼ cup all-purpose flour
- Salt and black pepper, to taste
- 1 pound of chicken breasts, cut into strips
- 2 tablespoons of oil bay seasoning
- oil spray, for greasing

Directions:
1. Take a medium bowl and whisk eggs with buttermilk.
2. In a separate large bowl mix flour, cornmeal, salt, black pepper, and oil bay seasoning.
3. First, dip the chicken breast strip in egg wash and then dredge into the flour mixture.
4. Coat the strip all over and layer on both the baskets that are already grease with oil spray.
5. Grease the chicken breast strips with oil spray as well.
6. Set the zone 1 basket to AIR FRY mode at 400 degrees F for 22 minutes.
7. Select the MATCH button for zone 2.
8. Hit the start button to let the cooking start.
9. Once the cooking cycle is done, serve.

Nutrition:
- (Per serving) Calories 788| Fat25g| Sodium835 mg | Carbs60g | Fiber 4.9g | Sugar1.5g | Protein79g

Chapter 8: Fish And Seafood Recipes

Scallops Gratiné With Parmesan

Servings: 2
Cooking Time: 9 Minutes
Ingredients:

- Scallops:
- 120 ml single cream
- 45 g grated Parmesan cheese
- 235 g thinly sliced spring onions
- 5 g chopped fresh parsley
- 3 cloves garlic, minced
- ½ teaspoon kosher or coarse sea salt
- ½ teaspoon black pepper
- 455 g sea scallops
- Topping:
- 30 g panko bread crumbs
- 20 g grated Parmesan cheese
- Vegetable oil spray
- For Serving:
- Lemon wedges
- Crusty French bread (optional)

Directions:
1. For the scallops: In a baking pan, combine the single cream, cheese, spring onions, parsley, garlic, salt, and pepper. Stir in the scallops. 2. For the topping: In a small bowl, combine the bread crumbs and cheese. Sprinkle evenly over the scallops. Spray the topping with vegetable oil spray. 3. Place the pan in the zone 1 air fryer drawer. Set the temperature to 164°C for 6 minutes. Set the temperature to 204°C for 3 minutes until the topping has browned. 4. To serve: Squeeze the lemon wedges over the gratin and serve with crusty French bread, if desired.

Orange-mustard Glazed Salmon

Servings: 2
Cooking Time: 10 Minutes
Ingredients:

- 1 tablespoon orange marmalade
- ¼ teaspoon grated orange zest plus 1 tablespoon juice
- 2 teaspoons whole-grain mustard
- 2 (230 g) skin-on salmon fillets, 1½ inches thick
- Salt and pepper, to taste
- Vegetable oil spray

Directions:
1. Preheat the zone 1 air fryer drawer to 204°C.
2. Make foil sling for air fryer drawer by folding 1 long sheet of aluminum foil so it is 4 inches wide. Lay sheet of foil widthwise across drawer, pressing foil into and up sides of drawer. Fold excess foil as needed so that edges of foil are flush with top of drawer. Lightly spray foil and drawer with vegetable oil spray.
3. Combine marmalade, orange zest and juice, and mustard in bowl. Pat salmon dry with paper towels and season with salt and pepper. Brush tops and sides of fillets evenly with glaze. Arrange fillets skin side down on sling in prepared drawer, spaced evenly apart. Air fry salmon until center is still translucent when checked with the tip of a paring knife and registers 52°C, 10 to 14 minutes, using sling to rotate fillets halfway through cooking.
4. Using the sling, carefully remove salmon from air fryer. Slide fish spatula along underside of fillets and transfer to individual serving plates, leaving skin behind. Serve.

Cajun Catfish Cakes With Cheese

Servings: 4
Cooking Time: 35 Minutes
Ingredients:

- 2 catfish fillets
- 85 g butter
- 150 g shredded Parmesan cheese
- 150 g shredded Swiss cheese
- 120 ml buttermilk
- 1 teaspoon baking powder
- 1 teaspoon baking soda
- 1 teaspoon Cajun seasoning

Directions:
1. Bring a pot of salted water to a boil. Add the catfish fillets to the boiling water and let them boil for 5 minutes until they become opaque.

2. Remove the fillets from the pot to a mixing bowl and flake them into small pieces with a fork.
3. Add the remaining ingredients to the bowl of fish and stir until well incorporated.
4. Divide the fish mixture into 12 equal portions and shape each portion into a patty.
5. Preheat the air fryer to 190ºC.
6. Arrange the patties in the two air fryer baskets and air fry for 15 minutes until golden brown and cooked through. Flip the patties halfway through the cooking time.
7. Let the patties sit for 5 minutes and serve.

Lemony Prawns And Courgette

Servings: 4
Cooking Time: 7 To 8 Minutes
Ingredients:
- 570 g extra-large raw prawns, peeled and deveined
- 2 medium courgettes (about 230 g each), halved lengthwise and cut into ½-inch-thick slices
- 1½ tablespoons olive oil
- ½ teaspoon garlic salt
- 1½ teaspoons dried oregano
- ⅛ teaspoon crushed red pepper flakes (optional)
- Juice of ½ lemon
- 1 tablespoon chopped fresh mint
- 1 tablespoon chopped fresh dill

Directions:
1. Preheat the air fryer to 176ºC.
2. In a large bowl, combine the prawns, courgette, oil, garlic salt, oregano, and pepper flakes and toss to coat.
3. Arrange a single layer of the prawns and courgette in the two air fryer drawers. Air fry for 7 to 8 minutes, shaking the drawer halfway, until the courgette is golden and the prawns are cooked through.
4. Transfer to a serving dish and tent with foil while you air fry the remaining prawns and courgette.
5. Top with the lemon juice, mint, and dill and serve.

Flavorful Salmon Fillets

Servings: 2
Cooking Time: 10 Minutes
Ingredients:
- 2 salmon fillets, boneless
- 1/2 tsp garlic powder
- 1/2 tsp ground cumin
- 1/2 tsp chili powder
- 2 tbsp fresh lemon juice
- 2 tbsp olive oil
- Pepper
- Salt

Directions:
1. In a small bowl, mix oil, lemon juice, chili powder, ground cumin, garlic powder, pepper, and salt.
2. Brush salmon fillets with oil mixture and place into the air fryer basket and cook at 400 F for 10 minutes.
3. Serve and enjoy.

Bacon Halibut Steak

Servings: 4
Cooking Time: 10 Minutes
Ingredients:
- 680 g halibut steaks (170 g each fillet)
- 1 teaspoon avocado oil
- 1 teaspoon ground black pepper
- 110 g bacon, sliced

Directions:
1. Sprinkle the halibut steaks with avocado oil and ground black pepper.
2. Then wrap the fish in the bacon slices and put in the two air fryer baskets.
3. Cook the fish at 200ºC for 5 minutes per side.

Chili Lime Tilapia

Servings: 4
Cooking Time: 10 Minutes
Ingredients:
- 340g tilapia fillets
- 2 teaspoons chili powder
- 1 teaspoon cumin
- 1 teaspoon garlic powder
- ½ teaspoon oregano
- ½ teaspoon sea salt
- ¼ teaspoon black pepper
- Lime zest from 1 lime
- Juice of ½ lime

Directions:
1. Mix chili powder and other spices with lime juice and zest in a bowl.
2. Rub this spice mixture over the tilapia fillets.
3. Place two fillets in each air basket.
4. Return the air fryer basket to the Ninja Foodi 2 Baskets Air Fryer.
5. Choose the "Air Fry" mode for Zone 1 at 400 degrees F and 10 minutes of cooking time.
6. Select the "MATCH COOK" option to copy the settings for Zone 2.
7. Initiate cooking by pressing the START/PAUSE BUTTON.
8. Flip the tilapia fillets once cooked halfway through.
9. Serve warm.

Nutrition:
- (Per serving) Calories 275 | Fat 1.4g | Sodium 582mg | Carbs 31.5g | Fiber 1.1g | Sugar 0.1g | Protein 29.8g

Keto Baked Salmon With Pesto

Servings: 2
Cooking Time: 18
Ingredients:
- 4 salmon fillets, 2 inches thick
- 2 ounces green pesto
- Salt and black pepper
- ½ tablespoon of canola oil, for greasing
- 1-1/2 cup mayonnaise
- 2 tablespoons Greek yogurt
- Salt and black pepper, to taste

Directions:
1. Rub the salmon with pesto, salt, oil, and black pepper.
2. In a small bowl, whisk together all the green sauce ingredients.
3. Divide the fish fillets between both the baskets.
4. Set zone 1 to air fry mode for 18 minutes at 390 degrees F.
5. Select MATCH button for Zone 2 basket.
6. Once the cooking is done, serve it with green sauce drizzle.
7. Enjoy.

Nutrition:
- (Per serving) Calories 1165 | Fat 80.7 g | Sodium 1087 mg | Carbs 33.1g | Fiber 0.5g | Sugar 11.5 g | Protein 80.6g

Fish Cakes

Servings: 4
Cooking Time: 10 To 12 Minutes
Ingredients:
- 1 large russet potato, mashed
- 340 g cod or other white fish
- Salt and pepper, to taste
- Olive or vegetable oil for misting or cooking spray
- 1 large egg
- 50 g potato starch
- 60 g panko breadcrumbs
- 1 tablespoon fresh chopped chives
- 2 tablespoons minced onion

Directions:
1. Peel potatoes, cut into cubes, and cook on stovetop till soft.
2. Salt and pepper raw fish to taste. Mist with oil or cooking spray, and air fry at 182°C for 6 to 8 minutes, until fish flakes easily. If fish is crowded, rearrange halfway through cooking to ensure all pieces cook evenly.
3. Transfer fish to a plate and break apart to cool.
4. Beat egg in a shallow dish.
5. Place potato starch in another shallow dish, and panko crumbs in a third dish.
6. When potatoes are done, drain in colander and rinse with cold water.
7. In a large bowl, mash the potatoes and stir in the chives and onion. Add salt and pepper to taste, then stir in the fish.
8. If needed, stir in a tablespoon of the beaten egg to help bind the mixture.
9. Shape into 8 small, fat patties. Dust lightly with potato starch, dip in egg, and roll in panko crumbs. Spray both sides with oil or cooking spray.
10. Air fry for 10 to 12 minutes, until golden brown and crispy.

Broiled Crab Cakes With Hush Puppies

Servings: 4
Cooking Time: 15 Minutes
Ingredients:
- FOR THE CRAB CAKES
- 2 large eggs
- 2 tablespoons Dijon mustard
- 2 teaspoons Worcestershire sauce
- 1 teaspoon Old Bay seasoning
- ¼ teaspoon paprika
- ¼ cup cracker crumbs (about 9 crackers)
- 1 pound lump crab meat
- 2 teaspoons vegetable oil

- FOR THE HUSH PUPPIES
- ½ cup all-purpose flour
- ⅓ cup yellow cornmeal
- 3 tablespoons sugar
- ¼ teaspoon kosher salt
- ¼ teaspoon baking powder
- 1 large egg
- ½ cup whole milk
- Nonstick cooking spray

Directions:
1. To prep the crab cakes: In a large bowl, whisk together the eggs, mustard, Worcestershire, Old Bay, and paprika until smooth. Stir in the cracker crumbs until fully incorporated, then fold in the crab meat. Refrigerate the crab mixture for 30 minutes.
2. Divide the crab mixture into 8 equal portions. With damp hands, press each portion gently into a loose patty. Brush both sides of each patty with the oil.
3. To prep the hush puppies: In a large bowl, combine the flour, cornmeal, sugar, salt, and baking powder. Stir in the egg and milk to form a stiff batter.
4. Roll the batter into 8 balls. Spritz each hush puppy with cooking spray.
5. To cook the crab cakes and hush puppies: Install a crisper plate in each of the two baskets. Place the crab cakes in a single layer in the Zone 1 basket and insert the basket in the unit. Line the Zone 2 plate with aluminum foil and spray the foil with cooking spray. Arrange the hush puppies on the foil and insert the basket in the unit.
6. Select Zone 1, select AIR BROIL, set the temperature to 400°F, and set the timer to 15 minutes.
7. Select Zone 2, select AIR FRY, set the temperature to 400°F, and set the timer to 7 minutes. Select SMART FINISH.
8. Press START/PAUSE to begin cooking.
9. When cooking is complete, the crab cakes and hush puppies will be golden brown and cooked through. Serve hot.

Nutrition:
- (Per serving) Calories: 403; Total fat: 16g; Saturated fat: 2g; Carbohydrates: 40g; Fiber: 1g; Protein: 27g; Sodium: 872mg

Salmon Patties

Servings: 8
Cooking Time: 18 Minutes.

Ingredients:

- 1 lb. fresh Atlantic salmon side
- ¼ cup avocado, mashed
- ¼ cup cilantro, diced
- 1 ½ teaspoons yellow curry powder
- ½ teaspoons sea salt
- ¼ cup, 4 teaspoons tapioca starch
- 2 brown eggs
- ½ cup coconut flakes
- Coconut oil, melted, for brushing
- For the greens:
- 2 teaspoons organic coconut oil, melted
- 6 cups arugula & spinach mix, tightly packed
- Pinch of sea salt

Directions:

1. Remove the fish skin and dice the flesh.
2. Place in a large bowl. Add cilantro, avocado, salt, and curry powder mix gently.
3. Add tapioca starch and mix well again.
4. Make 8 salmon patties out of this mixture, about a half-inch thick.
5. Place them on a baking sheet lined with wax paper and freeze them for 20 minutes.
6. Place ¼ cup tapioca starch and coconut flakes on a flat plate.
7. Dip the patties in the whisked egg, then coat the frozen patties in the starch and flakes.
8. Place half of the patties in each of the crisper plate and spray them with cooking oil
9. Return the crisper plate to the Ninja Foodi Dual Zone Air Fryer.
10. Choose the Air Fry mode for Zone 1 and set the temperature to 390 degrees F and the time to 17 minutes.
11. Select the "MATCH" button to copy the settings for Zone 2.
12. Initiate cooking by pressing the START/STOP button.
13. Flip the patties once cooked halfway through, then resume cooking.
14. Sauté arugula with spinach in coconut oil in a pan for 30 seconds.
15. Serve the patties with sautéed greens mixture

Nutrition:

- (Per serving) Calories 260 | Fat 16g |Sodium 585mg | Carbs 3.1g | Fiber 1.3g | Sugar 0.2g | Protein 25.5g

"fried" Fish With Seasoned Potato Wedges

Servings:4
Cooking Time: 30 Minutes

Ingredients:

- FOR THE FISH
- 4 cod fillets (6 ounces each)
- 4 tablespoons all-purpose flour, divided
- ¼ cup cornstarch
- 1 teaspoon baking powder
- ¼ teaspoon kosher salt
- ⅓ cup lager-style beer or sparkling water
- Tartar sauce, cocktail sauce, or malt vinegar, for serving (optional)
- FOR THE POTATOES
- 4 russet potatoes
- 2 tablespoons vegetable oil
- ½ teaspoon paprika
- ½ teaspoon kosher salt
- ¼ teaspoon garlic powder
- ¼ teaspoon freshly ground black pepper

Directions:

1. To prep the fish: Pat the fish dry with a paper towel and coat lightly with 2 tablespoons of flour.
2. In a shallow dish, combine the remaining 2 tablespoons of flour, the cornstarch, baking powder, and salt. Stir in the beer to form a thick batter.
3. Dip the fish in the batter to coat both sides, then let rest on a cutting board for 10 minutes.
4. To prep the potatoes: Cut each potato in half lengthwise, then cut each half into 4 wedges.

5. In a large bowl, combine the potatoes and oil. Toss well to fully coat the potatoes. Add the paprika, salt, garlic powder, and black pepper and toss well to coat.
6. To cook the fish and potato wedges: Install a crisper plate in each of the two baskets. Place a piece of parchment paper or aluminum foil over the plate in the Zone 1 basket. Place the fish in the basket and insert the basket in the unit. Place the potato wedges in a single layer in the Zone 2 basket and insert the basket in the unit.
7. Select Zone 1, select AIR FRY, set the temperature to 400°F, and set the timer to 13 minutes.
8. Select Zone 2, select AIR FRY, set the temperature to 400°F, and set the timer to 30 minutes. Select SMART FINISH.
9. Press START/PAUSE to begin cooking.
10. When the Zone 1 timer reads 5 minutes, press START/PAUSE. Remove the basket and use a silicone spatula to carefully flip the fish over. Reinsert the basket and press START/PAUSE to resume cooking.
11. When cooking is complete, the fish should be cooked through and the potatoes crispy outside and tender inside. Serve hot with tartar sauce, cocktail sauce, or malt vinegar (if using).

Nutrition:
- (Per serving) Calories: 360; Total fat: 8g; Saturated fat: 1g; Carbohydrates: 40g; Fiber: 2g; Protein: 30g; Sodium: 302mg

Garlic Butter Salmon

Servings: 4
Cooking Time: 10 Minutes

Ingredients:
- 4 (6-ounce) boneless, skin-on salmon fillets (preferably wild-caught)
- 4 tablespoons butter, melted
- 2 teaspoons garlic, minced
- 2 teaspoons fresh Italian parsley, chopped (or ¼ teaspoon dried)
- Salt and pepper to taste

Directions:
1. Season the fresh salmon with salt and pepper.
2. Mix together the melted butter, garlic, and parsley in a bowl.
3. Baste the salmon fillets with the garlic butter mixture.
4. Place a crisper plate in each drawer. Put 2 fillets in each drawer. Put the drawers inside the unit.
5. Select zone 1, then AIR FRY, then set the temperature to 360 degrees F/ 180 degrees C with a 10-minute timer. To match zone 2 settings to zone 1, choose MATCH. To begin, select START/STOP.
6. Remove the salmon from the drawers after the timer has finished.

Nutrition:
- (Per serving) Calories 338 | Fat 26g | Sodium 309mg | Carbs 1g | Fiber 0g | Sugar 0g | Protein 25g

Nutty Prawns With Amaretto Glaze

Servings: 10 To 12
Cooking Time: 10 Minutes

Ingredients:
- 120 g plain flour
- ½ teaspoon baking powder
- 1 teaspoon salt
- 2 eggs, beaten
- 120 ml milk
- 2 tablespoons olive or vegetable oil
- 185 g sliced almonds
- 900 g large prawns (about 32 to 40 prawns), peeled and deveined, tails left on
- 470 ml amaretto liqueur

Directions:
1. Combine the flour, baking powder and salt in a large bowl. Add the eggs, milk and oil and stir until it forms a smooth batter. Coarsely crush the sliced almonds into a second shallow dish with your hands.
2. Dry the prawns well with paper towels. Dip the prawns into the batter and shake off any excess batter, leaving just enough to lightly coat the prawns. Transfer the prawns to the dish with the almonds and coat completely. Place the coated prawns on a plate or baking sheet and when all the prawns have been coated, freeze the prawns for an 1 hour, or as long as a week before air frying.

3. Preheat the air fryer to 204°C.
4. Transfer frozen prawns to the two air fryer drawers. Air fry for 6 minutes. Turn the prawns over and air fry for an additional 4 minutes.
5. While the prawns are cooking, bring the Amaretto to a boil in a small saucepan on the stovetop. Lower the heat and simmer until it has reduced and thickened into a glaze, about 10 minutes.
6. Remove the prawns from the air fryer and brush both sides with the warm amaretto glaze. Serve warm.

Rainbow Salmon Kebabs And Tuna Melt

Servings: 3
Cooking Time: 10 Minutes
Ingredients:
- Rainbow Salmon Kebabs:
- 170 g boneless, skinless salmon, cut into 1-inch cubes
- ¼ medium red onion, peeled and cut into 1-inch pieces
- ½ medium yellow bell pepper, seeded and cut into 1-inch pieces
- ½ medium courgette, trimmed and cut into ½-inch slices
- 1 tablespoon olive oil
- ½ teaspoon salt
- ¼ teaspoon ground black pepper
- Tuna Melt:
- Olive or vegetable oil, for spraying
- 140 g can tuna, drained
- 1 tablespoon mayonnaise
- ¼ teaspoon garlic granules, plus more for garnish
- 2 teaspoons unsalted butte
- 2 slices sandwich bread of choice
- 2 slices Cheddar cheese

Directions:
1. Make the Rainbow Salmon Kebabs : Using one skewer, skewer 1 piece salmon, then 1 piece onion, 1 piece bell pepper, and finally 1 piece courgette. Repeat this pattern with additional skewers to make four kebabs total. Drizzle with olive oil and sprinkle with salt and black pepper. 2. Place kebabs into the ungreased zone 1 air fryer drawer. Adjust the temperature to 204°C and air fry for 8 minutes, turning kebabs halfway through cooking. Salmon will easily flake and have an internal temperature of at least 64°C when done; vegetables will be tender. Serve warm.
2. Make the Tuna Melt : 1. Line the zone 2 air fryer drawer with baking paper and spray lightly with oil. In a medium bowl, mix together the tuna, mayonnaise, and garlic. 3. Spread 1 teaspoon of butter on each slice of bread and place one slice butter-side down in the prepared drawer. 4. Top with a slice of cheese, the tuna mixture, another slice of cheese, and the other slice of bread, butter-side up. 5. Air fry at 204°C for 5 minutes, flip, and cook for another 5 minutes, until browned and crispy. 6. Sprinkle with additional garlic, before cutting in half and serving.

Furikake Salmon

Servings: 4
Cooking Time: 10 Minutes
Ingredients:
- ½ cup mayonnaise
- 1 tablespoon shoyu
- 455g salmon fillet
- Salt and black pepper to taste
- 2 tablespoons furikake

Directions:
1. Mix shoyu with mayonnaise in a small bowl.
2. Rub the salmon with black pepper and salt.
3. Place the salmon pieces in the air fryer baskets.
4. Top them with the mayo mixture.
5. Return the air fryer basket 1 to Zone 1, and basket 2 to Zone 2 of the Ninja Foodi 2-Basket Air Fryer.
6. Choose the "Air Fry" mode for Zone 1 at 400 degrees F and 10 minutes of cooking time.
7. Select the "MATCH COOK" option to copy the settings for Zone 2.
8. Initiate cooking by pressing the START/PAUSE BUTTON.
9. Serve warm.

Nutrition:
- (Per serving) Calories 297 | Fat 1g | Sodium 291mg | Carbs 35g | Fiber 1g | Sugar 9g | Protein 29g

Honey Teriyaki Salmon

Servings: 3
Cooking Time: 12 Minutes

Ingredients:
- 8 tablespoon teriyaki sauce
- 3 tablespoons honey
- 2 cubes frozen garlic
- 2 tablespoons olive oil
- 3 pieces wild salmon

Directions:
1. Mix teriyaki sauce, honey, garlic and oil in a large bowl.
2. Add salmon to this sauce and mix well to coat.
3. Cover and refrigerate the salmon for 20 minutes.
4. Place the salmon pieces in one air fryer basket.
5. Return the air fryer basket 1 to Zone 1 of the Ninja Foodi 2-Basket Air Fryer.
6. Choose the "Air Fry" mode for Zone 1 and set the temperature to 350 degrees F and 12 minutes of cooking time.
7. Initiate cooking by pressing the START/PAUSE BUTTON.
8. Flip the pieces once cooked halfway through.
9. Serve warm.

Nutrition:
- (Per serving) Calories 260 | Fat 16g |Sodium 585mg | Carbs 3.1g | Fiber 1.3g | Sugar 0.2g | Protein 25.5g

Perfect Parmesan Salmon

Servings: 4
Cooking Time:10 Minutes

Ingredients:
- 4 salmon fillets
- 1/4 cup parmesan cheese, shredded
- 1/4 tsp dried dill
- 1/2 tbsp Dijon mustard
- 4 tbsp mayonnaise
- 1 lemon juice
- Pepper
- Salt

Directions:
1. In a small bowl, mix cheese, dill, mustard, mayonnaise, lemon juice, pepper, and salt.
2. Place salmon fillets into the air fryer basket and brush with cheese mixture.
3. Cook salmon fillets at 400 F for 10 minutes.
4. Serve and enjoy.

Steamed Cod With Garlic And Swiss Chard

Servings: 4
Cooking Time: 12 Minutes

Ingredients:
- 1 teaspoon salt
- ½ teaspoon dried oregano
- ½ teaspoon dried thyme
- ½ teaspoon garlic powder
- 4 cod fillets
- ½ white onion, thinly sliced
- 135 g Swiss chard, washed, stemmed, and torn into pieces
- 60 ml olive oil
- 1 lemon, quartered

Directions:
1. Preheat the air fryer to 192ºC.
2. In a small bowl, whisk together the salt, oregano, thyme, and garlic powder.
3. Tear off four pieces of aluminum foil, with each sheet being large enough to envelop one cod fillet and a quarter of the vegetables.
4. Place a cod fillet in the middle of each sheet of foil, then sprinkle on all sides with the spice mixture.

5. In each foil packet, place a quarter of the onion slices and 30 g Swiss chard, then drizzle 1 tablespoon olive oil and squeeze ¼ lemon over the contents of each foil packet.
6. Fold and seal the sides of the foil packets and then place them into the two air fryer drawers. Steam for 12 minutes.
7. Remove from the drawers, and carefully open each packet to avoid a steam burn.

Basil Cheese S·saltalmon

Servings: 4
Cooking Time: 7 Minutes
Ingredients:
- 4 salmon fillets
- 1/4 cup parmesan cheese, grated
- 5 fresh basil leaves, minced
- 2 tbsp mayonnaise
- 1/2 lemon juice
- Pepper

Directions:
1. Preheat the air fryer to 400 F.
2. Brush salmon fillets with lemon juice and season with pepper and salt.
3. In a small bowl, mix mayonnaise, basil, and cheese.
4. Spray air fryer basket with cooking spray.
5. Place salmon fillets into the air fryer basket and brush with mayonnaise mixture and cook for 7 minutes.
6. Serve and enjoy.

Honey Teriyaki Tilapia

Servings: 4
Cooking Time: 10 Minutes
Ingredients:
- 8 tablespoons low-sodium teriyaki sauce
- 3 tablespoons honey
- 2 garlic cloves, minced
- 2 tablespoons extra virgin olive oil
- 3 pieces tilapia (each cut into 2 pieces)

Directions:
1. Combine all the first 4 ingredients to make the marinade.
2. Pour the marinade over the tilapia and let it sit for 20 minutes.
3. Place a crisper plate in each drawer. Place the tilapia in the drawers. Insert the drawers into the unit.
4. Select zone 1, then AIR FRY, then set the temperature to 360 degrees F/ 180 degrees C with a 10-minute timer. To match zone 2 settings to zone 1, choose MATCH. To begin, select START/STOP.
5. Remove the tilapia from the drawers after the timer has finished.

Nutrition:
- (Per serving) Calories 350 | Fat 16.4g | Sodium 706mg | Carbs 19.3g | Fiber 0.1g | Sugar 19g | Protein 29.3g

Cod With Avocado And Garlic Prawns

Servings: 5
Cooking Time: 10 Minutes
Ingredients:
- Cod with Avocado:
- 90 g shredded cabbage
- 60 ml full-fat sour cream
- 2 tablespoons full-fat mayonnaise
- 20 g chopped pickled jalapeños
- 2 (85 g) cod fillets
- 1 teaspoon chilli powder
- 1 teaspoon cumin
- ½ teaspoon paprika
- ¼ teaspoon garlic powder
- 1 medium avocado, peeled, pitted, and sliced
- ½ medium lime
- Garlic Prawns:
- Prawns:
- Olive or vegetable oil, for spraying
- 450 g medium raw prawns, peeled and deveined
- 6 tablespoons unsalted butter, melted
- 120 g panko bread crumbs
- 2 tablespoons garlic granules
- 1 teaspoon salt
- ½ teaspoon freshly ground black pepper
- Garlic Butter Sauce:

The Complete Ninja Foodi Dual Zone Air Fryer Cookbook

- 115 g unsalted butter
- 2 teaspoons garlic granules
- ¾ teaspoon salt (omit if using salted butter)

Directions:
1. Make the Cod with Avocado :
2. In a large bowl, place cabbage, sour cream, mayonnaise, and jalapeños. Mix until fully coated. Let sit for 20 minutes in the refrigerator.
3. Sprinkle cod fillets with chilli powder, cumin, paprika, and garlic powder. Place each fillet into the zone 1 air fryer drawer.
4. Adjust the temperature to 188ºC and set the timer for 10 minutes.
5. Flip the fillets halfway through the cooking time. When fully cooked, fish should have an internal temperature of at least 64ºC.
6. To serve, divide slaw mixture into two serving bowls, break cod fillets into pieces and spread over the bowls, and top with avocado. Squeeze lime juice over each bowl. Serve immediately.
7. Make the Garlic Prawns :
8. Make the Prawns
9. Preheat the air fryer to 204ºC. Line the zone 2 air fryer drawer with baking paper and spray lightly with oil.
10. Place the prawns and melted butter in a zip-top plastic bag, seal, and shake well, until evenly coated.
11. In a medium bowl, mix together the breadcrumbs, garlic, salt, and black pepper.
12. Add the prawns to the panko mixture and toss until evenly coated. Shake off any excess coating.
13. Place the prawns in the prepared drawer and spray lightly with oil.
14. Cook for 8 to 10 minutes, flipping and spraying with oil after 4 to 5 minutes, until golden brown and crispy. Make the Garlic Butter Sauce
15. In a microwave-safe bowl, combine the butter, garlic, and salt and microwave on 50% power for 30 to 60 seconds, stirring every 15 seconds, until completely melted.
16. Serve the prawns immediately with the garlic butter sauce on the side for dipping.

Beer Battered Fish Fillet

Servings:2
Cooking Time:14
Ingredients:
- 1 cup all-purpose flour
- 4 tablespoons cornstarch
- 1 teaspoon baking soda
- 8 ounces beer
- 2 egg beaten
- ½ cup all-purpose flour
- 1 teaspoon smoked paprika
- 1 teaspoon salt
- 1/4 teaspoon freshly ground black pepper
- ¼ teaspoon of cayenne pepper
- 2 cod fillets, 1½-inches thick, cut into 4 pieces
- Oil spray, for greasing

Directions:
1. Take a large bowl and combine flour, baking soda, corn starch, and salt
2. In a separate bowl beat eggs along with the beer.
3. In a shallow dish mix paprika, salt, pepper, and cayenne pepper.
4. Dry the codfish fillets with a paper towel.
5. Dip the fish into the eggs and coat it with seasoned flour.
6. Then dip it in the seasoning.
7. Grease the fillet with oil spray.
8. Divide the fillet between both zones.
9. Set zone 1 to AIR FRY mode at 400 degrees F for 14 minutes.
10. Select MACTH button for zone 2 basket.
11. Press start and let the AIR fry do its magic.
12. Once cooking is done, serve the fish.
13. Enjoy it hot.

Nutrition:
- (Per serving) Calories 1691| Fat 6.1g| Sodium 3976mg | Carbs105.1 g | Fiber 3.4g | Sugar15.6 g | Protein 270g

Easy Herbed Salmon

Servings: 2
Cooking Time: 5 Minutes

Ingredients:
- 2 salmon fillets
- 1 tbsp butter
- 2 tbsp olive oil
- 1/4 tsp paprika
- 1 tsp herb de Provence
- Pepper
- Salt

Directions:
1. Brush salmon fillets with oil and sprinkle with paprika, herb de Provence, pepper, and salt.
2. Place salmon fillets into the air fryer basket and cook at 390 F for 5 minutes.
3. Melt butter in a pan and pour over cooked salmon fillets.
4. Serve and enjoy.

Oyster Po'boy

Servings: 4
Cooking Time: 5 Minutes

Ingredients:
- 105 g plain flour
- 40 g yellow cornmeal
- 1 tablespoon Cajun seasoning
- 1 teaspoon salt
- 2 large eggs, beaten
- 1 teaspoon hot sauce
- 455 g pre-shucked oysters
- 1 (12-inch) French baguette, quartered and sliced horizontally
- Tartar Sauce, as needed
- 150 g shredded lettuce, divided
- 2 tomatoes, cut into slices
- Cooking spray

Directions:
1. In a shallow bowl, whisk the flour, cornmeal, Cajun seasoning, and salt until blended. In a second shallow bowl, whisk together the eggs and hot sauce.
2. One at a time, dip the oysters in the cornmeal mixture, the eggs, and again in the cornmeal, coating thoroughly.
3. Preheat the zone 1 air fryer drawer to 204ºC. Line the zone 1 air fryer drawer with baking paper.
4. Place the oysters on the baking paper and spritz with oil.
5. Air fry for 2 minutes. Shake the drawer, spritz the oysters with oil, and air fry for 3 minutes more until lightly browned and crispy.
6. Spread each sandwich half with Tartar Sauce. Assemble the po'boys by layering each sandwich with fried oysters, ½ cup shredded lettuce, and 2 tomato slices.
7. Serve immediately.

Seafood Shrimp Omelet

Servings: 2
Cooking Time: 15

Ingredients:
- 6 large shrimp, shells removed and chopped
- 6 eggs, beaten
- ½ tablespoon of butter, melted
- 2 tablespoons green onions, sliced
- 1/3 cup of mushrooms, chopped
- 1 pinch paprika
- Salt and black pepper, to taste
- Oil spray, for greasing

Directions:
1. In a large bowl whisk the eggs and add chopped shrimp, butter, green onions, mushrooms, paprika, salt, and black pepper.
2. Take two cake pans that fit inside the air fryer and grease them with oil spray.
3. Pour the egg mixture between the cake pans and place it in two baskets of the air fryer.

4. Turn on the BAKE function of zone 1, and let it cook for 15 minutes at 320 degrees F.
5. Select the MATCH button to match the cooking time for the zone 2 basket.
6. Once the cooking cycle completes, take out, and serve hot.

Nutrition:
- (Per serving) Calories 300 | Fat 17.5g| Sodium 368mg | Carbs 2.9g | Fiber 0.3g | Sugar1.4 g | Protein32.2 g

Crispy Parmesan Cod

Servings: 2
Cooking Time: 10 Minutes

Ingredients:
- 455g cod filets
- Salt and black pepper, to taste
- ½ cup flour
- 2 large eggs, beaten
- ½ teaspoon salt
- 1 cup Panko
- ½ cup grated parmesan
- 2 teaspoons old bay seasoning
- ½ teaspoon garlic powder
- Olive oil spray

Directions:
1. Rub the cod fillets with black pepper and salt.
2. Mix panko with parmesan cheese, old bay seasoning, and garlic powder in a bowl.
3. Mix flour with salt in another bowl.
4. Dredge the cod filets in the flour then dip in the eggs and coat with the Panko mixture.
5. Place the cod fillets in the air fryer baskets.
6. Return the air fryer basket 1 to Zone 1, and basket 2 to Zone 2 of the Ninja Foodi 2-Basket Air Fryer.
7. Choose the "Air Fry" mode for Zone 1 and set the temperature to 400 degrees F and 10 minutes of cooking time.
8. Select the "MATCH COOK" option to copy the settings for Zone 2.
9. Initiate cooking by pressing the START/PAUSE BUTTON.
10. Flip the cod fillets once cooked halfway through.
11. Serve warm.

Nutrition:
- (Per serving) Calories 275 | Fat 1.4g |Sodium 582mg | Carbs 31.5g | Fiber 1.1g | Sugar 0.1g | Protein 29.8g

Pecan-crusted Catfish

Servings: 4
Cooking Time: 12 Minutes

Ingredients:
- 65 g pecans, finely crushed
- 1 teaspoon fine sea salt
- ¼ teaspoon ground black pepper
- 4 catfish fillets, 110g each
- For Garnish (Optional):
- Fresh oregano
- Pecan halves

Directions:
1. Spray the two air fryer drawers with avocado oil. Preheat the air fryer to 192°C.
2. In a large bowl, mix the crushed pecan, salt, and pepper. One at a time, dredge the catfish fillets in the mixture, coating them well. Use your hands to press the pecan meal into the fillets. Spray the fish with avocado oil and place them in the two air fryer drawers.
3. Air fry the coated catfish for 12 minutes, or until it flakes easily and is no longer translucent in the center, flipping halfway through.
4. Garnish with oregano sprigs and pecan halves, if desired.
5. Store leftovers in an airtight container in the fridge for up to 3 days. Reheat in a preheated 176°C air fryer for 4 minutes, or until heated through.

Salmon Nuggets

Servings: 4
Cooking Time: 15 Minutes.

Ingredients:
- ⅓ cup maple syrup
- ¼ teaspoon dried chipotle pepper
- 1 pinch sea salt
- 1 ½ cups croutons
- 1 large egg
- 1 (1 pound) skinless salmon fillet, cut into 1 ½-inch chunk
- cooking spray

Directions:
1. Mix chipotle powder, maple syrup, and salt in a saucepan and cook on a simmer for 5 minutes.
2. Crush the croutons in a food processor and transfer to a bowl.
3. Beat egg in another shallow bowl.
4. Season the salmon chunks with sea salt.
5. Dip the salmon in the egg, then coat with breadcrumbs.
6. Divide the coated salmon chunks in the two crisper plates.
7. Return the crisper plate to the Ninja Foodi Dual Zone Air Fryer.
8. Select the Air Fry mode for Zone 1 and set the temperature to 390 degrees F and the time to 10 minutes.
9. Press the "MATCH" button to copy the settings for Zone 2.
10. Initiate cooking by pressing the START/STOP button.
11. Flip the chunks once cooked halfway through, then resume cooking.
12. Pour the maple syrup on top and serve warm.

Nutrition:
- (Per serving) Calories 275 | Fat 1.4g |Sodium 582mg | Carbs 31.5g | Fiber 1.1g | Sugar 0.1g | Protein 29.8g

Buttered Mahi-mahi

Servings: 4
Cooking Time: 22 Minutes.

Ingredients:
- 4 (6-oz) mahi-mahi fillets
- Salt and black pepper ground to taste
- Cooking spray
- ⅔ cup butter

Directions:
1. Preheat your Ninja Foodi Dual Zone Air Fryer to 350 degrees F.
2. Rub the mahi-mahi fillets with salt and black pepper.
3. Place two mahi-mahi fillets in each of the crisper plate.
4. Return the crisper plates to the Ninja Foodi Dual Zone Air Fryer.
5. Choose the Air Fry mode for Zone 1 and set the temperature to 390 degrees F and the time to 17 minutes.
6. Select the "MATCH" button to copy the settings for Zone 2.
7. Initiate cooking by pressing the START/STOP button.
8. Add butter to a saucepan and cook for 5 minutes until slightly brown.
9. Remove the butter from the heat.
10. Drizzle butter over the fish and serve warm.

Nutrition:
- (Per serving) Calories 399 | Fat 16g |Sodium 537mg | Carbs 28g | Fiber 3g | Sugar 10g | Protein 35g

Chapter 9: Desserts Recipes

Churros

Servings: 8
Cooking Time: 10 Minutes

Ingredients:
- 1 cup water
- 1/3 cup unsalted butter, cut into cubes
- 2 tablespoons granulated sugar
- ¼ teaspoon salt
- 1 cup all-purpose flour
- 2 large eggs
- 1 teaspoon vanilla extract
- Cooking oil spray
- For the cinnamon-sugar coating:
- ½ cup granulated sugar
- ¾ teaspoon ground cinnamon

Directions:
1. Add the water, butter, sugar, and salt to a medium pot. Bring to a boil over medium-high heat.
2. Reduce the heat to medium-low and stir in the flour. Cook, stirring constantly with a rubber spatula until the dough is smooth and comes together.
3. Remove the dough from the heat and place it in a mixing bowl. Allow 4 minutes for cooling.
4. In a mixing bowl, beat the eggs and vanilla extract with an electric hand mixer or stand mixer until the dough comes together. The finished product will resemble gluey mashed potatoes. Press the lumps together into a ball with your hands, then transfer to a large piping bag with a large star-shaped tip. Pipe out the churros.
5. Install a crisper plate in both drawers. Place half the churros in the zone 1 drawer and half in zone 2's, then insert the drawers into the unit.
6. Select zone 1, select AIR FRY, set temperature to 390 degrees F/ 200 degrees C, and set time to 12 minutes. Select MATCH to match zone 2 settings to zone 1. Press the START/STOP button to begin cooking.
7. In a shallow bowl, combine the granulated sugar and cinnamon.
8. Immediately transfer the baked churros to the bowl with the sugar mixture and toss to coat.

Nutrition:
- (Per serving) Calories 204 | Fat 9g | Sodium 91mg | Carbs 27g | Fiber 0.3g | Sugar 15g | Protein 3g

Fluffy Layered Peanut Butter Cheesecake Brownies

Servings: 6
Cooking Time: 35 Minutes

Ingredients:
- ½ cup blanched finely ground almond flour
- 1 cup powdered erythritol, divided
- 2 tablespoons unsweetened cocoa powder
- ½ teaspoon baking powder
- ¼ cup unsalted butter, softened
- 2 large eggs, divided
- 8 ounces full-fat cream cheese, softened
- ¼ cup heavy whipping cream
- 1 teaspoon vanilla extract
- 2 tablespoons no-sugar-added peanut butter

Directions:
1. In a large bowl, combine ½ cup erythritol, almond flour, baking powder and cocoa powder. Add in butter and one egg, stir well.
2. Spoon mixture into 6" round baking pan. Put pan into the air fryer basket.
3. Set the temperature to 300°F, then set the timer for 20 minutes.
4. A toothpick inserted in center will come out clean when fully cooked. Allow to completely cool for 20 minutes and firm up.
5. In a large bowl, beat heavy cream, cream cheese, remaining ½ cup erythritol, peanut butter, remaining egg, and vanilla until turns fluffy.
6. Spoon mixture over cooled brownies. Return the pan into the air fryer basket.
7. Set the temperature to 300°F, then set the timer for 15 minutes.
8. When fully done, cheesecake will be slightly browned and mostly firm with
9. a slight jiggle. Let it rest and refrigerate for at least 2 hours before serving.

Fried Cheesecake Bites

Servings: 16 Bites
Cooking Time: 2 Minutes

Ingredients:
- 225 g cream cheese, softened
- 50 g powdered sweetener, plus 2 tablespoons, divided
- 4 tablespoons heavy cream, divided
- ½ teaspoon vanilla extract
- 50 g almond flour

Directions:
1. In a stand mixer fitted with a paddle attachment, beat the cream cheese, 50 g of the sweetener, 2 tablespoons of the heavy cream, and the vanilla until smooth. Using a small ice-cream scoop, divide the mixture into 16 balls and arrange them on a rimmed baking sheet lined with baking paper. Freeze for 45 minutes until firm.
2. Line the two air fryer drawers with baking paper and preheat the air fryer to 176ºC.
3. In a small shallow bowl, combine the almond flour with the remaining 2 tablespoons of sweetener.
4. In another small shallow bowl, place the remaining 2 tablespoons cream.
5. One at a time, dip the frozen cheesecake balls into the cream and then roll in the almond flour mixture, pressing lightly to form an even coating. Arrange the balls in a single layer in the two air fryer drawers, leaving room between them. Air fry for 2 minutes until the coating is lightly browned.

Lemon Sugar Cookie Bars Monster Sugar Cookie Bars

Servings: 12
Cooking Time: 18 Minutes

Ingredients:
- FOR THE LEMON COOKIE BARS
- Grated zest and juice of 1 lemon
- ½ cup granulated sugar
- 4 tablespoons (½ stick) unsalted butter, at room temperature
- 1 large egg yolk
- 1 teaspoon vanilla extract
- ⅛ teaspoon baking powder
- ½ cup plus 2 tablespoons all-purpose flour
- FOR THE MONSTER COOKIE BARS
- ½ cup granulated sugar
- 4 tablespoons (½ stick) unsalted butter, at room temperature
- 1 large egg yolk
- 1 teaspoon vanilla extract
- ⅛ teaspoon baking powder
- ½ cup plus 2 tablespoons all-purpose flour
- ¼ cup rolled oats
- ¼ cup M&M's
- ¼ cup peanut butter chips

Directions:
1. To prep the lemon cookie bars: In a large bowl, rub together the lemon zest and sugar. Add the butter and use a hand mixer to beat until light and fluffy.
2. Beat in the egg yolk, vanilla, and lemon juice. Mix in the baking powder and flour.
3. To prep the monster cookie bars: In a large bowl, with a hand mixer, beat the sugar and butter until light and fluffy.
4. Beat in the egg yolk and vanilla. Mix in the baking powder and flour. Stir in the oats, M&M's, and peanut butter chips.
5. To cook the cookie bars: Line both baskets with aluminum foil. Press the lemon cookie dough into the Zone 1 basket and insert the basket in the unit. Press the monster cookie dough into the Zone 2 basket and insert the basket in the unit.
6. Select Zone 1, select BAKE, set the temperature to 330°F, and set the timer to 18 minutes. Press MATCH COOK to match Zone 2 settings to Zone 1.
7. Press START/PAUSE to begin cooking.
8. When cooking is complete, the cookies should be set in the middle and have begun to pull away from the sides of the basket.
9. Let the cookies cool completely, about 1 hour. Cut each basket into 6 bars for a total of 12 bars.

Nutrition:
- (Per serving) Calories: 191; Total fat: 8.5g; Saturated fat: 5g; Carbohydrates: 27g; Fiber: 0.5g; Protein: 2g; Sodium: 3mg

Olive Oil Cake & Old-fashioned Fudge Pie

Servings: 16
Cooking Time: 30 Minutes
Ingredients:
- Olive Oil Cake:
- 120 g blanched finely ground almond flour
- 5 large eggs, whisked
- 175 ml extra-virgin olive oil
- 75 g granulated sweetener
- 1 teaspoon vanilla extract
- 1 teaspoon baking powder
- Old-Fashioned Fudge Pie:
- 300 g granulated sugar
- 40 g unsweetened cocoa powder
- 70 g self-raising flour
- 3 large eggs, unbeaten
- 12 tablespoons unsalted butter, melted
- 1½ teaspoons vanilla extract
- 1 (9-inch) unbaked piecrust
- 30 g icing sugar (optional)

Directions:
1. Make the Olive Oil Cake :
2. In a large bowl, mix all ingredients. Pour batter into an ungreased round nonstick baking dish.
3. Place dish into the zone 1 air fryer basket. Adjust the temperature to 150°C and bake for 30 minutes. The cake will be golden on top and firm in the center when done.
4. Let cake cool in dish 30 minutes before slicing and serving.
5. Make the Old-Fashioned Fudge Pie :
6. In a medium bowl, stir together the sugar, cocoa powder, and flour. Stir in the eggs and melted butter. Stir in the vanilla.
7. Preheat the air fryer to 175°C.
8. Pour the chocolate filing into the crust.
9. Cook in the zone 2 basket for 25 to 30 minutes, stirring every 10 minutes, until a knife inserted into the middle comes out clean. Let sit for 5 minutes before dusting with icing sugar to serve.

Mini Blueberry Pies

Servings: 2
Cooking Time: 10
Ingredients:
- 1 box Store-Bought Pie Dough, Trader Joe's
- ¼ cup blueberry jam
- 1 teaspoon of lemon zest
- 1 egg white, for brushing

Directions:
1. Take the store brought pie dough and cut it into 3-inch circles.
2. Brush the dough with egg white all around the parameters.
3. Now add blueberry jam and zest in the middle and top it with another circular.
4. Press the edges with the fork to seal it.
5. Make a slit in the middle of the dough and divide it between the baskets.
6. Set zone 1 to AIR FRY mode 360 degrees for 10 minutes.
7. Select the MATCH button for zone 2.
8. Once cooked, serve.

Nutrition:
- (Per serving) Calories 234| Fat8.6g| Sodium187 mg | Carbs 38.2 g | Fiber 0.1g | Sugar13.7 g | Protein 2g

Walnuts Fritters

Servings: 6
Cooking Time: 15 Minutes.
Ingredients:
- 1 cup all-purpose flour
- ½ cup walnuts, chopped
- ¼ cup white sugar
- ¼ cup milk

- 1 egg
- 1 ½ teaspoons baking powder
- 1 pinch salt
- Cooking spray
- 2 tablespoons white sugar
- ½ teaspoon ground cinnamon
- Glaze:
- ½ cup confectioners' sugar
- 1 tablespoon milk
- ½ teaspoon caramel extract
- ¼ teaspoons ground cinnamon

Directions:
1. Layer both crisper plate with parchment paper.
2. Grease the parchment paper with cooking spray.
3. Whisk flour with milk, ¼ cup of sugar, egg, baking powder, and salt in a small bowl.
4. Separately mix 2 tablespoons of sugar with cinnamon in another bowl, toss in walnuts and mix well to coat.
5. Stir in flour mixture and mix until combined.
6. Drop the fritters mixture using a cookie scoop into the two crisper plate.
7. Return the crisper plate to the Ninja Foodi Dual Zone Air Fryer.
8. Choose the Air Fry mode for Zone 1 and set the temperature to 375 degrees F and the time to 15 minutes.
9. Select the "MATCH" button to copy the settings for Zone 2.
10. Initiate cooking by pressing the START/STOP button.
11. Flip the fritters once cooked halfway through, then resume cooking.
12. Meanwhile, whisk milk, caramel extract, confectioners' sugar, and cinnamon in a bowl.
13. Transfer fritters to a wire rack and allow them to cool.
14. Drizzle with a glaze over the fritters.

Nutrition:
- (Per serving) Calories 391 | Fat 24g | Sodium 142mg | Carbs 38.5g | Fiber 3.5g | Sugar 21g | Protein 6.6g

Jelly Donuts

Servings: 4
Cooking Time: 5 Minutes

Ingredients:
- 1 package Pillsbury Grands (Homestyle)
- ½ cup seedless raspberry jelly
- 1 tablespoon butter, melted
- ½ cup sugar

Directions:
1. Install a crisper plate in both drawers. Place half of the biscuits in the zone 1 drawer and half in zone 2's, then insert the drawers into the unit. You may need to cook in batches.
2. Select zone 1, select AIR FRY, set temperature to 390 degrees F/ 200 degrees C, and set time to 22 minutes. Select MATCH to match zone 2 settings to zone 1. Press the START/STOP button to begin cooking.
3. Place the sugar into a wide bowl with a flat bottom.
4. Baste all sides of the cooked biscuits with the melted butter and roll in the sugar to cover completely.
5. Using a long cake tip, pipe 1–2 tablespoons of raspberry jelly into each biscuit. You've now got raspberry-filled donuts!

Nutrition:
- (Per serving) Calories 252 | Fat 7g | Sodium 503mg | Carbs 45g | Fiber 0g | Sugar 23g | Protein 3g

Sweet Protein Powder Doughnut Holes

Servings: 6 (2 Per Serving)
Cooking Time: 6 Minutes

Ingredients:
- ½ cup blanched finely ground almond flour
- ½ cup low-carb vanilla protein powder
- ½ cup granular erythritol
- ½ teaspoon baking powder
- 1 large egg
- 5 tablespoons unsalted butter, melted
- ½ teaspoon vanilla extract

Directions:

1. Stir all ingredients well in a large bowl. Put into the freezer for at least 20 minutes.
2. Wet your hands with water, then form the dough into 12 balls with your hands.
3. Slice a sheet of parchment which fit your air fryer basket. Handling in batches if needed, put doughnut holes into the air fryer basket onto the parchment.
4. Set the temperature to 380°F, then set the timer for 6 minutes.
5. Turn doughnut holes over halfway through the cooking time.
6. Allow them to cool fully before serving.

Strawberry Nutella Hand Pies

Servings: 8
Cooking Time: 10 Minutes
Ingredients:
- 1 tube pie crust dough
- 3–4 strawberries, finely chopped
- Nutella
- Sugar
- Coconut oil cooking spray

Directions:
1. Roll out the pie dough and place it on a baking sheet. Cut out hearts using a 3-inch heart-shaped cookie cutter as precisely as possible.
2. Gather the leftover dough into a ball and roll it out thinly to make a few more heart shapes. For 8 hand pies, I was able to get 16 hearts from one tube of pie crust.
3. Set aside a baking tray lined with parchment paper.
4. Spread a dollop of Nutella (approximately 1 teaspoon) on one of the hearts. Add a few strawberry pieces to the mix. Add a pinch of sugar to the top.
5. Place another heart on top and use a fork to tightly crimp the edges. Gently poke holes in the top of the pie with a fork. Place on a baking sheet. Repeat for all the pies.
6. All of the pies on the tray should be sprayed with coconut oil.
7. Install a crisper plate in both drawers. Place half the pies in the zone 1 drawer and half in zone 2's, then insert the drawers into the unit.
8. Select zone 1, select BAKE, set temperature to 390 degrees F/ 200 degrees C, and set time to 10 minutes. Select MATCH to match zone 2 settings to zone 1. Press the START/STOP button to begin cooking.

Nutrition:
- (Per serving) Calories 41 | Fat 2.1g | Sodium 18mg | Carbs 5.5g | Fiber 0.4g | Sugar 4.1g | Protein 0.4g

Fruity Blackberry Crisp

Servings: 4
Cooking Time: 15 Minutes
Ingredients:
- 2 cups blackberries
- ⅓ cup powdered erythritol
- 2 tablespoons lemon juice
- ¼ teaspoon xanthan gum
- 1 cup Crunchy Granola

Directions:
1. Mix erythritol, blackberries, xanthan gum, and lemon juice in a large bowl.
2. Place into 6" round baking dish and cover with a sheet of foil. Put into the air fryer basket.
3. Set the temperature to 350°F, then set the timer for 12 minutes.
4. When the goes off, remove the foil and shake well.
5. Sprinkle granola on the top of mixture and place back to the air fryer basket.
6. Set the temperature to 320°F, then set the timer for 3 minutes or until the top is golden brown.
7. Serve immediately.

Victoria Sponge Cake

Servings: 8
Cooking Time: 16 Minutes

Ingredients:

- Sponge Cake Ingredients
- 400g self-rising flour
- 450g caster sugar
- 50g lemon curd
- 200g butter
- 4 medium eggs
- 1 tablespoon vanilla essence
- 480ml skimmed milk
- 1 tablespoon olive oil
- 4 tablespoons strawberry jam
- Strawberry buttercream
- 115g butter
- 210g icing sugar
- ½ teaspoon strawberry food coloring
- 1 tablespoon single cream
- 1 teaspoon vanilla essence
- 1 teaspoon maple syrup

Directions:

1. Mix sugar and butter in a bowl using a hand mixer.
2. Beat eggs with oil, and vanilla in a bowl with the mixer until creamy.
3. Stir in milk, flour and curd then mix well.
4. Add butter mixture then mix well.
5. Divide this mixture in two 4 inches greased cake pans.
6. Place one pan in each air fryer basket.
7. Return the air fryer basket 1 to Zone 1, and basket 2 to Zone 2 of the Ninja Foodi 2-Basket Air Fryer.
8. Choose the "Air Fry" mode for Zone 1 and set the temperature to 375 degrees F and 16 minutes of cooking time.
9. Select the "MATCH COOK" option to copy the settings for Zone 2.
10. Initiate cooking by pressing the START/PAUSE BUTTON.
11. Meanwhile, blend the buttercream ingredients in a mixer until fluffy.
12. Place one cake on a plate and top it with the buttercream.
13. Top it jam and then with the other cake.
14. Serve.

Nutrition:

- (Per serving) Calories 284 | Fat 16g | Sodium 252mg | Carbs 31.6g | Fiber 0.9g | Sugar 6.6g | Protein 3.7g

Apple Crumble

Servings: 4
Cooking Time: 30 Minutes

Ingredients:

- 1 can apple pie filling
- 6 tablespoons caster sugar
- 8 tablespoons self-rising flour
- ¼ cup butter, softened
- A pinch of salt

Directions:

1. Take a baking dish.
2. Arrange apple pie filling evenly into the prepared baking dish.
3. Take a large bowl, add all the remaining ingredients. Mix well.
4. Place the mixture evenly all over apple pie filling.
5. Press "Zone 1" and "Zone 2" and then rotate the knob for each zone to select "Bake".
6. Set the temperature to 320 degrees F/ 160 degrees C for both zones and then set the time for 5 minutes to preheat.
7. After preheating, arrange the baking dish into the basket of each zone.
8. Slide each basket into Air Fryer and set the time for 25 minutes.
9. After cooking time is completed, remove the baking dish from Air Fryer.
10. Set aside to cool.
11. Serve and enjoy!

Dessert Empanadas

Servings: 12
Cooking Time: 10 Minutes

Ingredients:
- 12 empanada wrappers thawed
- 2 apples, chopped
- 2 tablespoons raw honey
- 1 teaspoon vanilla extract
- 1 teaspoon cinnamon
- ⅛ teaspoon nutmeg
- 2 teaspoons cornstarch
- 1 teaspoon water
- 1 egg beaten

Directions:
1. Mix apples with vanilla, honey, nutmeg, and cinnamon in a saucepan.
2. Cook for 3 minutes then mix cornstarch with water and pour into the pan.
3. Cook for 30 seconds.
4. Allow this filling to cool and keep it aside.
5. Spread the wrappers on the working surface.
6. Divide the apple filling on top of the wrappers.
7. Fold the wrappers in half and seal the edges by pressing them.
8. Brush the empanadas with the beaten egg and place them in the air fryer basket 1.
9. Return the air fryer basket 1 to Zone 1 of the Ninja Foodi 2-Basket Air Fryer.
10. Choose the "Air Fry" mode for Zone 1 at 400 degrees F and 10 minutes of cooking time.
11. Initiate cooking by pressing the START/PAUSE BUTTON.
12. Flip the empanadas once cooked halfway through.
13. Serve.

Nutrition:
- (Per serving) Calories 204 | Fat 9g |Sodium 91mg | Carbs 27g | Fiber 2.4g | Sugar 15g | Protein 1.3g

Chocolate Chip Pecan Biscotti

Servings: 10
Cooking Time: 20 To 22 Minutes

Ingredients:
- 135 g finely ground blanched almond flour
- ¾ teaspoon baking powder
- ½ teaspoon xanthan gum
- ¼ teaspoon sea salt
- 3 tablespoons unsalted butter, at room temperature
- 35 g powdered sweetener
- 1 large egg, beaten
- 1 teaspoon pure vanilla extract
- 50 g chopped pecans
- 40 g organic chocolate chips,
- Melted organic chocolate chips and chopped pecans, for topping (optional)

Directions:
1. In a large bowl, combine the almond flour, baking powder, xanthan gum, and salt.
2. Line a cake pan that fits inside your air fryer with baking paper.
3. In the bowl of a stand mixer, beat together the butter and powdered sweetener. Add the beaten egg and vanilla and beat for about 3 minutes.
4. Add the almond flour mixture to the butter and egg mixture; beat until just combined.
5. Stir in the pecans and chocolate chips.
6. Transfer the dough to the prepared pan and press it into the bottom.
7. Set the air fryer to 165ºC and bake for 12 minutes. Remove from the air fryer and let cool for 15 minutes. Using a sharp knife, cut the cookie into thin strips, then return the strips to the cake pan with the bottom sides facing up.
8. Set the air fryer to 150ºC. Bake for 8 to 10 minutes.
9. Remove from the air fryer and let cool completely on a wire rack. If desired, dip one side of each biscotti piece into melted chocolate chips, and top with chopped pecans.

Pumpkin Cookie With Cream Cheese Frosting

Servings: 6
Cooking Time: 7 Minutes
Ingredients:

- 50 g blanched finely ground almond flour
- 50 g powdered sweetener, divided
- 2 tablespoons butter, softened
- 1 large egg
- ½ teaspoon unflavored gelatin
- ½ teaspoon baking powder
- ½ teaspoon vanilla extract
- ½ teaspoon pumpkin pie spice
- 2 tablespoons pure pumpkin purée
- ½ teaspoon ground cinnamon, divided
- 40 g low-carb, sugar-free chocolate chips
- 85 g full-fat cream cheese, softened

Directions:
1. In a large bowl, mix almond flour and 25 gsweetener. Stir in butter, egg, and gelatin until combined. 2. Stir in baking powder, vanilla, pumpkin pie spice, pumpkin purée, and ¼ teaspoon cinnamon, then fold in chocolate chips. 3. Pour batter into a round baking pan. Place pan into the zone 1 air fryer basket. 4. Adjust the temperature to 150°C and bake for 7 minutes. 5. When fully cooked, the top will be golden brown, and a toothpick inserted in center will come out clean. Let cool at least 20 minutes. 6. To make the frosting: mix cream cheese, remaining ¼ teaspoon cinnamon, and remaining 25 g sweetener in a large bowl. Using an electric mixer, beat until it becomes fluffy. Spread onto the cooled cookie. Garnish with additional cinnamon if desired.

Stuffed Apples

Servings: 8
Cooking Time: 10 Minutes
Ingredients:

- 8 small firm apples, cored
- 1 cup golden raisins
- 1 cup blanched almonds
- 4 tablespoons sugar
- ¼ teaspoon ground cinnamon

Directions:
1. In a food processor, add raisins, almonds, sugar and cinnamon and pulse until chopped.
2. Carefully stuff each apple with raisin mixture.
3. Line each basket of "Zone 1" and "Zone 2" with parchment paper.
4. Press "Zone 1" and "Zone 2" and then rotate the knob for each zone to select "Air Fry".
5. Set the temperature to 355 degrees F/ 180 degrees C for both zones and then set the time for 5 minutes to preheat.
6. After preheating, arrange 4 apples into the basket of each zone.
7. Slide each basket into Air Fryer and set the time for 10 minutes.
8. After cooking time is completed, remove the apples from Air Fryer.
9. Transfer the apples onto plates and set aside to cool slightly before serving.

Oreo Rolls

Servings: 9
Cooking Time: 8 Minutes.
Ingredients:

- 1 crescent sheet roll
- 9 Oreo cookies
- Cinnamon powder, to serve
- Powdered sugar, to serve

Directions:
1. Spread the crescent sheet roll and cut it into 9 equal squares.
2. Place one cookie at the center of each square.
3. Wrap each square around the cookies and press the ends to seal.
4. Place half of the wrapped cookies in each crisper plate.
5. Return the crisper plates to the Ninja Foodi Dual Zone Air Fryer.
6. Select the Bake mode for Zone 1 and set the temperature to 360 degrees F and the time to 4-6 minutes.

7. Select the "MATCH" button to copy the settings for Zone 2.
8. Initiate cooking by pressing the START/STOP button.
9. Check for the doneness of the cookie rolls if they are golden brown, else cook 1-2 minutes more.
10. Garnish the rolls with sugar and cinnamon.
11. Serve.

Nutrition:
- (Per serving) Calories 175 | Fat 13.1g | Sodium 154mg | Carbs 14g | Fiber 0.8g | Sugar 8.9g | Protein 0.7g

Chocolate And Rum Cupcakes

Servings: 6
Cooking Time: 15 Minutes

Ingredients:
- 150 g granulated sweetener
- 140 g almond flour
- 1 teaspoon unsweetened baking powder
- 3 teaspoons cocoa powder
- ½ teaspoon baking soda
- ½ teaspoon ground cinnamon
- ¼ teaspoon grated nutmeg
- ⅛ teaspoon salt
- 120 ml milk
- 110 g butter, at room temperature
- 3 eggs, whisked
- 1 teaspoon pure rum extract
- 70 g blueberries
- Cooking spray

Directions:
1. Preheat the air fryer to 175ºC. Spray a 6-cup muffin tin with cooking spray.
2. In a mixing bowl, combine the sweetener, almond flour, baking powder, cocoa powder, baking soda, cinnamon, nutmeg, and salt and stir until well blended.
3. In another mixing bowl, mix together the milk, butter, egg, and rum extract until thoroughly combined. Slowly and carefully pour this mixture into the bowl of dry mixture. Stir in the blueberries.
4. Spoon the batter into the greased muffin cups, filling each about three-quarters full.
5. Bake for 15 minutes, or until the center is springy and a toothpick inserted in the middle comes out clean.
6. Remove from the basket and place on a wire rack to cool. Serve immediately.

Coconut Muffins And Dark Chocolate Lava Cake

Servings: 9
Cooking Time: 25 Minutes

Ingredients:
- Coconut Muffins:
- 55 g coconut flour
- 2 tablespoons cocoa powder
- 3 tablespoons granulated sweetener
- 1 teaspoon baking powder
- 2 tablespoons coconut oil
- 2 eggs, beaten
- 50 g desiccated coconut
- Dark Chocolate Lava Cake:
- Olive oil cooking spray
- 30 g whole wheat flour
- 1 tablespoon unsweetened dark chocolate cocoa powder
- ⅛ teaspoon salt
- ½ teaspoon baking powder
- 60 ml raw honey
- 1 egg
- 2 tablespoons olive oil

Directions:
1. Make the Coconut Muffins :
2. In the mixing bowl, mix all ingredients.
3. Then pour the mixture into the molds of the muffin and transfer in the zone 1 air fryer basket.
4. Cook the muffins at 175ºC for 25 minutes.
5. Make the Dark Chocolate Lava Cake :
6. Preheat the air fryer to 190ºC. Lightly coat the insides of four ramekins with olive oil cooking spray.
7. In a medium bowl, combine the flour, cocoa powder, salt, baking powder, honey, egg, and olive oil.

8. Divide the batter evenly among the ramekins.
9. Place the filled ramekins inside the zone 2 air fryer basket and bake for 10 minutes.
10. Remove the lava cakes from the air fryer and slide a knife around the outside edge of each cake. Turn each ramekin upside down on a saucer and serve.

Baked Brazilian Pineapple

Servings: 4
Cooking Time: 10 Minutes
Ingredients:
- 95 g brown sugar
- 2 teaspoons ground cinnamon
- 1 small pineapple, peeled, cored, and cut into spears
- 3 tablespoons unsalted butter, melted

Directions:
1. In a small bowl, mix the brown sugar and cinnamon until thoroughly combined.
2. Brush the pineapple spears with the melted butter. Sprinkle the cinnamon-sugar over the spears, pressing lightly to ensure it adheres well.
3. Place the spears in the two air fryer drawers in a single layer. Set the air fryer to 204ºC and cook for 10 minutes. Halfway through the cooking time, brush the spears with butter.
4. The pineapple spears are done when they are heated through, and the sugar is bubbling. Serve hot.

Homemade Mint Pie And Strawberry Pecan Pie

Servings: 8
Cooking Time: 25 Minutes
Ingredients:
- Homemade Mint Pie:
- 1 tablespoon instant coffee
- 2 tablespoons almond butter, softened
- 2 tablespoons granulated sweetener
- 1 teaspoon dried mint
- 3 eggs, beaten
- 1 teaspoon dried spearmint
- 4 teaspoons coconut flour
- Cooking spray
- Strawberry Pecan Pie:
- 190 g whole shelled pecans
- 1 tablespoon unsalted butter, softened
- 240 ml heavy whipping cream
- 12 medium fresh strawberries, hulled
- 2 tablespoons sour cream

Directions:
1. Make the Homemade Mint Pie:
2. Spray the zone 1 air fryer drawer with cooking spray.
3. Then mix all ingredients in the mixer bowl.
4. When you get a smooth mixture, transfer it in the zone 1 air fryer drawer. Flatten it gently. Cook the pie at 185ºC for 25 minutes.
5. Make the Strawberry Pecan Pie:
6. Place pecans and butter into a food processor and pulse ten times until a dough forms. Press dough into the bottom of an ungreased round nonstick baking dish.
7. Place dish into the zone 2 air fryer drawer. Adjust the temperature to 160ºC and set the timer for 10 minutes. Crust will be firm and golden when done. Let cool 20 minutes.
8. In a large bowl, whisk cream until fluffy and doubled in size, about 2 minutes.
9. In a separate large bowl, mash strawberries until mostly liquid. Fold strawberries and sour cream into whipped cream.
10. Spoon mixture into cooled crust, cover, and place in refrigerator for at least 30 minutes to set. Serve chilled.

Homemade Mini Cheesecake

Servings: 2
Cooking Time: 15 Minutes
Ingredients:

- ½ cup walnuts
- 2 tablespoons salted butter
- 2 tablespoons granular erythritol
- 4 ounces full-fat cream cheese, softened
- 1 large egg
- ½ teaspoon vanilla extract
- ⅛ cup powdered erythritol

Directions:
1. Place butter, granular erythritol, and walnuts in a food processor. Pulse until all the ingredients stick together to form a dough.
2. Place dough into 4&quot| springform pan then put the pan into the air fryer basket.
3. Set the temperature to 400°F, then set the timer for 5 minutes.
4. When timer goes off, remove the crust and allow it rest.
5. Stir cream cheese with vanilla extract, powdered erythritol and egg until smooth in a medium bowl.
6. Pour mixture on top of baked walnut crust and then put into the air fryer basket.
7. Set the temperature to 300°F, then set the timer for 10 minutes.
8. Once cooked fully, allow to cool for 2 hours before serving.

S'mores Dip With Cinnamon-sugar Tortillas

Servings: 4
Cooking Time: 5 Minutes
Ingredients:

- FOR THE S'MORES DIP
- ½ cup chocolate-hazelnut spread
- ¼ cup milk chocolate or white chocolate chips
- ¼ cup graham cracker crumbs
- ½ cup mini marshmallows
- FOR THE CINNAMON-SUGAR TORTILLAS
- 4 (6-inch) flour tortillas
- Butter-flavored cooking spray
- 1 teaspoon granulated sugar
- ½ teaspoon ground cinnamon
- ¼ teaspoon ground cardamom (optional)

Directions:
1. To prep the s'mores dip: Spread the chocolate-hazelnut spread in the bottom of a shallow ovenproof ramekin or dish.
2. Scatter the chocolate chips and graham cracker crumbs over the top. Arrange the marshmallows in a single layer on top of the crumbs.
3. To prep the tortillas: Spray both sides of each tortilla with cooking spray. Cut each tortilla into 8 wedges and sprinkle both sides evenly with sugar, cinnamon, and cardamom (if using).
4. To cook the dip and tortillas: Install a crisper plate in each of the two baskets. Place the ramekin in the Zone 1 basket and insert the basket in the unit. Place the tortillas in the Zone 2 basket and insert the basket in the unit.
5. Select Zone 1, select BAKE, set the temperature to 330°F, and set the timer to 5 minutes.
6. Select Zone 2, select AIR FRY, set the temperature to 375°F, and set the timer to 5 minutes. Select SMART FINISH.
7. Press START/PAUSE to begin cooking.
8. When the Zone 2 timer reads 3 minutes, press START/PAUSE. Remove the basket and shake it to redistribute the chips. Reinsert the basket and press START/PAUSE to resume cooking.
9. When cooking is complete, the dip will be bubbling and golden brown and the chips crispy.
10. If desired, toast the marshmallows more: Select Zone 1, select AIR BROIL, set the temperature to 450°F, and set the timer to 1 minute. Cook until the marshmallows are deep golden brown.
11. Let the dip cool for 2 to 3 minutes. Serve with the cinnamon-sugar tortilla chips.

Nutrition:
- (Per serving) Calories: 404; Total fat: 18g; Saturated fat: 7g; Carbohydrates: 54g; Fiber: 2.5g; Protein: 6g; Sodium: 346mg

Grilled Peaches

Servings: 2
Cooking Time: 5 Minutes

Ingredients:
- 2 yellow peaches, peeled and cut into wedges
- ¼ cup graham cracker crumbs
- ¼ cup brown sugar
- ¼ cup butter diced into tiny cubes
- Whipped cream or ice cream

Directions:
1. Toss peaches with crumbs, brown sugar, and butter in a bowl.
2. Spread the peaches in one air fryer basket.
3. Return the air fryer basket to the Ninja Foodi 2 Baskets Air Fryer.
4. Choose the "Air Fry" mode for Zone 1 and set the temperature to 350 degrees F and 5 minutes of cooking time.
5. Initiate cooking by pressing the START/PAUSE BUTTON.
6. Serve the peaches with a scoop of ice cream.

Nutrition:
- (Per serving) Calories 327 | Fat 14.2g | Sodium 672mg | Carbs 47.2g | Fiber 1.7g | Sugar 24.8g | Protein 4.4g

Recipes Index

"fried" Chicken With Warm Baked Potato Salad 72
"fried" Fish With Seasoned Potato Wedges 79

A

Acorn Squash Slices 36
African Piri-piri Chicken Drumsticks 68
Almond Chicken 61
Asian Chicken Drumsticks 71
Asian Chicken 72
Avocado Fries 18
Air Fried Bacon And Eggs 28
Air Fried Chicken Potatoes With Sun-dried Tomato 67
Air Fried Okra 37
Air Fried Pot Stickers 21
Apricot-glazed Turkey Tenderloin 61
Apple Crumble 94

B

Bacon And Spinach Egg Muffins 26
Bacon Halibut Steak 76
Bacon Wrapped Pork Tenderloin 57
Bacon Potato Patties 36
Bacon, Cheese, And Avocado Melt & Cheesy Scrambled Eggs 26
Bacon-wrapped Cheese Pork 46
Baked Brazilian Pineapple 98
Baked Egg And Mushroom Cups 30
Baked Mushroom And Mozzarella Frittata With Breakfast Potatoes 25
Baked Peach Oatmeal 24
Balsamic Steak Tips With Roasted Asparagus And Mushroom Medley 52
Basil Cheese S·saltalmon 83
Bbq Corn 38
Beef And Bean Taquitos With Mexican Rice 48
Beef Jerky Pineapple Jerky 17
Beer Battered Fish Fillet 84
Blue Cheese Steak Salad 57
Blueberry Coffee Cake And Maple Sausage Patties 32
Bo Luc Lac 56
Brazilian Chicken Drumsticks 69
Breaded Pork Chops 52
Breakfast Stuffed Peppers 30
Breakfast Pitta 24
Broccoli, Squash, & Pepper 42

Broccoli-mushroom Frittata And Chimichanga Breakfast Burrito 33
Broiled Crab Cakes With Hush Puppies 78
Brussels Sprouts 36
Buffalo Bites 37
Buffalo Chicken Breakfast Muffins 30
Buffalo Seitan With Crispy Zucchini Noodles 43
Buttered Mahi-mahi 87
Buttermilk Biscuits With Roasted Stone Fruit Compote 25

C

Cajun Breakfast Sausage 29
Cajun Catfish Cakes With Cheese 75
Cajun Chicken With Vegetables 70
Cauliflower Cheese Patties 19
Caprese Panini With Zucchini Chips 37
Cheesy Baked Eggs 31
Chocolate And Rum Cupcakes 97
Chocolate Chip Pecan Biscotti 95
Churros 89
Chicken And Vegetable Fajitas 66
Chicken Breast Strips 73
Chicken Caprese 60
Chicken Leg Piece 70
Chicken Ranch Wraps 68
Chicken Stuffed Mushrooms 22
Chicken With Bacon And Tomato & Bacon-wrapped Stuffed Chicken Breasts 65
Chicken With Pineapple And Peach 60
Chili Chicken Wings 60
Chili Lime Tilapia 77
Coconut Muffins And Dark Chocolate Lava Cake 97
Cod With Avocado And Garlic Prawns 83
Crab Rangoon Dip With Crispy Wonton Strips 21
Crispy Dill Chicken Strips 64
Crispy Hash Browns 29
Crispy Parmesan Cod 86
Curried Orange Honey Chicken 66
Cinnamon Toast 33

D

Dessert Empanadas 95
Donuts 27

E

Easy Breaded Pork Chops 51

Easy Herbed Salmon 85
Easy Pancake Doughnuts 31
Egg And Bacon Muffins 24
Eggs In Avocado Cups 27

F

Flavorful Salmon Fillets 76
Fluffy Layered Peanut Butter Cheesecake Brownies 89
French Toasts 31
Fruity Blackberry Crisp 93
Fried Avocado Tacos 39
Fried Cheese 16
Fried Cheesecake Bites 90
Fried Patty Pan Squash 39
Furikake Salmon 81
Fish Cakes 77

G

Garlic Butter Salmon 80
Garlic Sirloin Steak 54
Garlic Parmesan Drumsticks 62
Garlic, Buffalo, And Blue Cheese Stuffed Chicken 71
Garlic-rosemary Pork Loin With Scalloped Potatoes And Cauliflower 50
Glazed Steak Recipe 46
Goat Cheese-stuffed Bavette Steak 47
Green Salad With Crispy Fried Goat Cheese And Baked Croutons 40
Grilled Peaches 100

H

Homemade Mint Pie And Strawberry Pecan Pie 98
Homemade Mini Cheesecake 99
Honey Teriyaki Salmon 82
Honey Teriyaki Tilapia 83

J

Jelly Donuts 92
Juicy Duck Breast 66
Juicy Pork Chops 53

K

Keto Baked Salmon With Pesto 77
Kheema Burgers 50
Kielbasa Sausage With Pineapple And Kheema Meatloaf 49

L

Lemon Sugar Cookie Bars Monster Sugar Cookie Bars 90
Lemony Pear Chips 20
Lemony Prawns And Courgette 76

M

Mac And Cheese Balls 20
Meatballs 51
Mongolian Beef With Sweet Chili Brussels Sprouts 45
Mozzarella Balls 15
Mozzarella Stuffed Beef And Pork Meatballs 55
Mozzarella Sticks 14
Minute Steak Roll-ups 53
Mini Blueberry Pies 91
Miso-glazed Shishito Peppers Charred Lemon Shishito Peppers 16

N

Nutty Prawns With Amaretto Glaze 80
Nigerian Peanut-crusted Bavette Steak 45

O

Olive Oil Cake & Old-fashioned Fudge Pie 91
Orange-mustard Glazed Salmon 75
Oreo Rolls 96
Oyster Po'boy 85

P

Parmesan French Fries 14
Parmesan Ranch Risotto And Oat And Chia Porridge .. 32
Parmesan Sausage Egg Muffins 29
Pecan-crusted Catfish 86
Perfect Cinnamon Toast 28
Perfect Parmesan Salmon 82
Potato Tacos 16
Potatoes Lyonnaise 27
Pretzel Chicken Cordon Bleu 64
Pumpkin Cookie With Cream Cheese Frosting 96
Pigs In A Blanket With Spinach-artichoke Stuffed Mushrooms 48

Q

Quinoa Patties 42

R

Ravioli 19
Rainbow Salmon Kebabs And Tuna Melt 81
Roast Souvlaki-style Pork With Lemon-feta Baby Potatoes 58
Roasted Beef 56
Roasted Garlic Chicken Pizza With Cauliflower "wings" 62
Rosemary And Garlic Lamb Chops 55

S

S'mores Dip With Cinnamon-sugar Tortillas 99

Salmon Nuggets 87
Salmon Patties 79
Satay-style Tempeh With Corn Fritters 41
Sausage And Cauliflower Arancini 47
Scallops Gratiné With Parmesan 75
Seafood Shrimp Omelet 85
Shrimp Pirogues 18
Steaks With Walnut-blue Cheese Butter 54
Steamed Cod With Garlic And Swiss Chard 82
Strawberry Nutella Hand Pies 93
Stuffed Apples 96
Stuffed Beef Fillet With Feta Cheese 46
Stuffed Chicken Florentine 65
Stuffed Tomatoes 39
Sweet And Spicy Carrots With Chicken Thighs 62
Sweet And Spicy Country-style Ribs 56
Sweet Protein Powder Doughnut Holes 92
Simple Lamb Meatballs 51

Spiced Chicken And Vegetables 67

T

Tasty Sweet Potato Wedges 14
Tasty Pork Skewers 54
Tater Tots 15
Thai Curry Meatballs 70
Tofu Veggie Meatballs 18
Turkey Meatloaf With Veggie Medley 63

V

Victoria Sponge Cake 94

W

Waffle Fries 22
Walnuts Fritters 91
Wings With Corn On The Cob 69

Printed in Great Britain
by Amazon